BEKEN
OF COWES

1 1897-1914

PHOTOGRAPHS BY FRANK AND KEITH BEKEN
TEXT BY JOHN CHAMIER
FOREWORD BY ALAIN GLIKSMAN

With an historical introduction and
colour plates from the Macpherson Collection in
the National Maritime Museum, Greenwich, London

CASSELL LONDON

CASSELL & COMPANY LTD, 35 Red Lion Square, London WCI
Melbourne, Sydney, Toronto, Johannesburg, Cape Town, Auckland

© Sté J.-L.-Roth et Cie 1966
First published in Great Britain 1966

Printed and bound in France

FOREWORD

OST of us take our heritage of sail too much as a matter of course—but perhaps not all. Perhaps some have taken thought of those who patiently forged this international language of sailing, developed the hulls, simplified the rigs—to bring yachts and yachting to the universal, practical sport and pastime it is today. Perhaps one day, in some misty Solent Creek or by some sunlit Long Island jetty, they will have come across a 'princess' of those earlier days—proud and dignified still, despite the rusty chains which bind her, the oil drums which litter her deck, the battered, smoking stovepipe and the clothes line full of washing. Perhaps there will have been on this scene an old white-bearded shellback who with a sweep of his hand will have cleared the horizon of all today's jostling dinghies, catamarans and cabin-cruisers, to bring back again the silent, but titanic battles of the years this book describes. Battles where Kings met to gain victory by a few feet or a few seconds, in an age when amongst so much that was ugly, all the beauty and *noblesse* in the world seems to have been poured into these lovely hulls and towering sails.

Now, when they are passing even beyond human memory, they can take shape again through the eyes of Frank Beken and his son Keith and through the words of John Chamier. Here, for all who love sea and sail, is the Grand Parade—the taut white wings of faultless sails, the splendours of polished brass and shining varnish, the hardy crews working their great ships as if their lives depended upon the outcome, the helmsmen and the owners with their gaze forever on the next mark.

Outside the covers of this book, these lovely craft and their men are now no more than dust. Frank and Keith Beken will save them from oblivion.

A.G.

3

IT BEGAN THUS....

It is tempting when we are looking for the source-springs of yachting, to call up Plutarch's description of the meeting of Anthony and Cleopatra. The Queen's barge is said to have proceeded to sea under sails of purple silk, her poop encrusted with gold and her banks of oars fashioned with finest silver. But from an historian's point of view this first recorded pleasure cruise must remain an embellishment of tall tales of long ago. In practice the oceans of the world were for century after century what they always had been—a stage for murder and violence, whereon some men ventured by reason of cupidity or constraint. Nations who now consider themselves steeped in seafaring tradition hardly existed in the Middle Ages.

Piracy was as much an occupation of gentlemen as of wicked barons—and a difference of nationality was never the only reason for one man plundering another. It was the commerce of greed and cruelty which prevailed.

Sea captains acknowledged no law but their own. Armed with 'letters of marque' or their equivalent, they sought to enrich themselves by sack and pillage of those who were weaker and on whom they could fix blame, however specious, to justify their attacks. The chronicles of the Middle Ages are full of accounts of punitive expeditions which of course provoked counter-attacks from the other parties as soon as they had had opportunity to recover. And so it went on.

At an international level no holds were barred. The laws of opposing countries only reached as far as low tide mark and there was certainly nothing which resembled an international agreement of right or wrong. Commercial shipping was more likely to fly the flag of a nobleman, or a city, or that of a league of merchants rather than the colours of a nation. In times of war the entire coastline of any country would be menaced by enemy expeditions. In times of peace, corsairs and pirates were only the more active. An English chronicler has recorded that before the middle of the seventeenth century no one knew the meaning of the word peace in English waters. It was not just the Mediterranean that was the 'property' of the Barbary pirates; they pushed farther afield and out into the Atlantic. After the establishment of the Moroccan port of Salé their expeditions northward redoubled in number. In 1631 Baltimore in Ireland was sacked and the inhabitants carried off into slavery. In 1640 the English vessel *Elizabeth* was attacked by three Turkish warships off the Lizard. She bested her opponents in a running fight which lasted eight hours. On her course to harbour and haven she encountered a number of small craft which had clearly been captured and whose crews were being held prisoner by the Turks.

In such conditions there can hardly have been room for seaborne cruising pleasures. Merchantmen were the only vessels to put to sea without intentions of violence. Fishermen from English as well as French ports seldom ventured beyond sight of their own coastlines.

However, by the end of the seventeenth century the Dutch were establishing a comfortable prosperity based on fishing. People were starting to say that Amsterdam itself was being built on herrings. The Dutch were well situated for the pursuit of commerce for their own well-being, protected as they were by their sandbanks, their shoals, their currents, their tides and their sea fogs. In fact, they created the first maritime nation in Europe and the world. Having done this they were also the first to use their maritime expertise for recreation and distraction upon their sheltered inland waters.

This is what made it possible for the Dutch East India Company to offer Charles II the 'yacht' which so excited the busy pen of Samuel Pepys. Englishmen were pleased enough to spectate at the activities of Charles II as the first British yachtsman—even though the king was forced soon enough to turn his pleasure yachts over to service in his Navy. Yet as early as 1646 the Stuart King, deprived of his throne and a refugee in the Scilly Isles, had occupied his enforced leisure with practical study of the art of sailing. When he reached the more secure shelter of Jersey he frequently took the helm during local sailing trips. On June 8 that year he took over a boat built to his ideas in Saint Malo. When he later reached Holland he was able to give free rein to his maritime aspirations.

However, although Charles cannot have owned fewer than twenty-eight boats and was certainly often enough at the helm in 'regattas' against the Duke of York and other personages, these were the distractions of a frivolous court and had as little to do with yachting as his descendants and we were to know it, as did the drinking bouts and other pastimes which followed. Such 'regattas' (the term was borrowed from the Venetians) were limited to London's river—and one must not forget that in 1667 the Dutch sailed up the Thames burning shipping as far as Chatham—on the King's front doorstep, as one might say.

In spite of royal patronage, yachting cannot at this stage be said to have become established. A more significant date perhaps is that of 1720. In this year was established the 'Water Club' at Cork, in Ireland. Members of the club could muster a squadron, even a fleet of vessels in the man-o'-war style. The 'fleet orders' and rules and regulations of this club are available to us in all their detail and complexity, although in the context of this book they are of little cogency. There is little of cruising or of racing in their content. The club's aim and purpose was the preservation of maritime tradition. This object was epitomised by an annual review in full style, surrounded by clouds of gunsmoke and the crash of cannon marking the signals and the salutes of a naval exercise. The 'Cork Water Club', which thereby achieved the enviable title of being the world's first established yacht club, died and was reborn a number of times between 1720 and our own times. Truth to tell, it played only a small part in a minor key in the birth of the sport of yachting. For that we must return to that sweet river, the Thames. From time to time vessels of transport and commerce engaged themselves in the hazards of direct competition. And in 1749 a dozen craft took part in an organised race from Greenwich to the Nore and back for a cup presented by the Prince of Wales, and shades of things to come, a vessel specially built for the event and entered in the name of *Princess Augusta* carried off the trophy. However, such activities were fairly haphazard and by 1754 the writer Henry Fielding was complaining that few of his contemporaries had much taste for the joys of sailing!

This was up-river stuff but things were not much livelier along the sea-coast. This is hardly surprising as here there existed a practically continuous state of warfare of one kind or another—and privateers from Dunkirk, for instance, were apt to skim off the cream of anything venturing on the waters of the Channel. Nevertheless one should not fail to take note of a three weeks cruise accomplished by Lord Ferrers in 1773—and a cross-Channel race and back accomplished in the same year by two chaloupes belonging to Lieutenants Friend and Columbine.

From this time forward we reach more established ground. In 1775 there was organised a regatta for seafaring craft starting at Ranelagh, the pleasure gardens on the site of the present Chelsea Hospital (now separated from real open water by no less than eleven bridges). In the same year the Duke of Cumberland put up a silver cup and this was the occasion of the birth of the Cumberland Sailing Society which in the course of time became the Royal Thames Yacht Club. In 1776 we find a painting by Serres of a regatta at Cowes, but in spite of the fact that the Channel was by now regarded as a reasonably secure waterway and England was generally at war only with her distant colonies, there were few enough yachts putting to sea. Security is only relative and in 1777 the *Hawk*, of the Cumberland Fleet, was pursued into the port of Calais itself by an American privateer.

Yachting as a sport continued to be domiciled for the most part between the banks of the Thames. In 1781 a contest for a cup presented by the Duke of Cumberland was opened to all sailing craft in the British Isles and their dominions. This and similar events were remarkable for the ferocity with which they were fought out. In 1786 rival competitors combined to obstruct a 'favourite' who disengaged herself by liberal use of the marline-spike and went on to win. In 1795 two competitors boarded each other, the skipper of the *Vixen* drawing his cutlass and cutting through the rigging of the *Mercury*, leaving her disabled.

However, during these years, among the modish frequenters of Cowes, there began to be found enthusiastic yachtsmen. In 1788 there was race at Cowes for yachts of under 35 tons measurement—with a prize of 30 guineas, worth £300 today.

In 1812 the first official regatta took place in the Isle of Wight and this was accompanied by a review of Trinity House pilots. A large number of yachtsmen took part in the racing—among them Lord Grantham, Mr. Fazackerly and Colonel Sheddon, whom we could have met three years later in a London tavern.

This was a meeting of some importance, for it was concerned with nothing less than the founding of an association which became the Royal Yacht Squadron—and a determining factor in the birth of a great international sport. But at that time the gathering consisted of gentlemen who loved sailing. Their 'club' was neither concerned with the numerical strength of its membership nor its wealth. Indeed the entrance fee was a few guineas and the minimum size of members' yachts was really very modest. There lacked only the actual existence of yachting as such and the evocative passion for the sea which has blossomed since then.

One of the founding members of this association was not present in person—he was very much engaged in losing a limb at the head of a British cavalry charge at

CUMBERLAND FLEET REGATTA

This is probably the first pictorial record of a regatta. In spite of slack rigging, eased sheets and formidable bowsprits, they beat up between the banks of a turbulent Thames. The vessel on the extreme right is having to bear away to allow a starboard tack yacht right of way. The mark itself cannot be far away—the booming out spars are already close up.

(Oil painting 1775.
Artist unknown.
Royal Thames Yacht Club.)

Waterloo! This small detail is not just an anecdote, for the 'Yacht Club' saw the light of day at the very dawn of a fantastic era of prosperity for England herself.

PEACE AT SEA

The year 1815 marked victory and the end of a dour and bloody struggle for Britain, and she went on to reap the fruits of this success. The fortunes of the few if not of the many rose with the prosperity of the British Isles.

For the rest of the world, the growing New as well as the exhausted Old, the year was significant for the appearance of a stable peace on the High Seas, the *pax Britannica*. Here then were the conditions which could produce a 'fleet of pleasure vessels'—peace at sea, and prosperity. The new sport was to develop with the dignity of the times and not the pace of today, and perhaps one cannot yet refer to its activities as a 'sport'. The driving idea behind the foundation of the Yacht Club was the formation of an association of high-born gentlemen professing an interest in things maritime. For the most part the ownership of a yacht was little more than aesthetic one-upmanship, and something aboard which one never went anywhere. The taboos and social exigencies of the day were carried so far as to discourage any over-close acquaintance with the actual conduct of the vessel. One elegant magazine, dispensing its advice to young yachtsmen, went so far as to recommend that its readers should not engage in discussion with the crew nor use maritime terminology.

But the most hot-blooded of these owners weren't content with merely possessing a splendid yacht. They wanted to have the best of the best. They proclaimed the virtues of their craft to the skies and defied anyone to prove the contrary. And that's how yacht-racing began, the product of the pride of owners —and the English passion for betting.

It would however be a mistake to see these contests as a pastime for the privileged. In this epoch sail was equally the propulsive power of the Royal Navy as it was of the merchant marine and the yachtsman. Each step of progress in any field was an authentic technical victory—and one achieved under the discipline which was at once the pride and the salvation of England. The handful of owners of yachts who fought their rather mannered contests were not only concerned to carry Britannia's new sport as high as they could; they were often also men of letters and science. When their vessels out-performed the Navy—or the Preventive men—the papers were loud is their criticism of sluggish bureaucracy in the Admiralty and the outdatedness of official ideas.

There was moreover something more. The peacetime reduction of the Royal Navy left thousands of competent seamen high and dry. These men, formed in a rough school by inclination or by the press-gangs, had but one trade and one asylum—the sea. Here then were ready-made crews composed of tough, hardened men, ready for hire and determined to carry the day to the point of severing an opponent's rigging with a cutlass at sea or to pursuing the contest ashore with their fists.

The chronicles of the day have meticulously preserved the names of the pioneers of the sport: like Lord Belfast,

COWES IN 1796

Deserted beaches, a bathing hut on wheels, and the least old fashioned of the remainder of the scene, the yachts. The house set back slightly from the shore is almost exactly on the site of the Royal Yacht Squadron.

(Aquatint. J. Hassell. Macpherson Collection.)

who one day in 1832 upped and followed an Admiralty brig as far as Portugal in order to give himself the satisfaction of racing and beating her in his *Waterwitch*. In 1826 the Marquis of Anglesey engaged his two vessels *Pearl* and *Liberty* against the *Arrow* and the *Julia* of Mr. Weld for a purse of £500—worth ten times that today, or more? 'If *Pearl* is beaten', announced Lord Anglesey, 'I'll burn her within the hour.' Happily enough she won her duel. *Liberty* lost hers and the match was declared 'all square'. Other vessels didn't have the *Pearl*'s luck and were despatched to the breakers after an unsuccessful season. In truth many if not all the founders of the Yacht Club were dedicated yachtsmen—men like Mr. J. Weld, owner of *Charlotte*, Lord Asheton Smith, owner of *Elizabeth*, and others like Mr. Sturt and Lord Bolton whose names appear frequently in the record of the following years.

In 1817 the Prince Regent became a member of the Yacht Club, which at this took the title of the Royal Yacht Club. Races became more frequent, but they were practically always due to the initiative of individuals and were most often in the form of match racing between two owners. Unfortunately, the simple sporting spirit of racing was often forgotten in the aftermath of the event itself, while the obscureness of the racing instructions was a forcing house for argument and accusations of cheating and the frequent collisions during a race itself were often settled by the use of knives against an opponent's rope rigging.

In 1826 the Royal Yacht Squadron went through the motions of properly organising racing for the first time, and in 1827 George IV signified his approval of this initiative by presenting a cup to mark the occasion. It is difficult to over-estimate the effect of this royal intervention. This first 'organised' race was hotly contested and saw Mr. Weld's *Lulworth* the victrix. However, it does not seem that the losers were prepared to accept their defeat with good grace. Almost immediately, Lord Belfast challenged the winner to race against his yacht *Louise* for a sum of 1,000 guineas —and incidentally won the wager. Two years later, in 1829, is recorded the Marquis of Anglesey's organisation of the regatta at Dublin.

IN SEARCH OF RULES FOR THE SPORT

But with this attempt to introduce orderliness into racing came the first difficulties—at this early stage!—with problems of measurement. To start with, yachts raced boat for boat on an elapsed time basis. Owners were quick to realise, as G.L. Watson was to say years later, that a good big 'un would beat a good little 'un. There was nothing surprising in the fact that the first crack racers were the biggest and costliest—*Arrow* displaced 84 tons, *Lulworth* 82, *Alarm* 193, and *Louise* 180.

It was soon abundantly clear that a 'rule for the game' would have to be found if competitive racing was not quickly to fade from the scene for lack of competitors. The idea of equalising everyone's chances at the start came easily to mind, but on what was it to be based? Length? It was possible to find so many very dissimilar craft with the same length or even with the same sail area. Then there were so many different rigs with their own varying degrees of complication. For that matter, at that time it was unimaginable that any rule should dictate the design or the construction of a yacht or the limits to which her designer and builder could go. The easiest way out was thought to be to base a rule on the system in force in the merchant marine for measuring vessels for tonnage dues. Initiated by Mr. Holland-Ackers, a complicated system was evolved based on elapsed time over the course distance related to the differences in size between competing craft. This could be termed the 'Rule of 94'.

CRUISE OF THE ROYAL YACHT SQUADRON TO CHERBOURG IN 1835

Falcon, the Earl of Yarborough's yacht—he was the first Commodore of the R.Y.S.—is enthroned in the middle of the fleet. She was a man o'war in miniature down to her guns and armament. (At which chandler's did one buy cannon in those days?) On either side of her are two famous vessels—the cutter Pearl *and the brig* Waterwitch.

(Aquatint. C. Rosenberg. Macpherson Collection.)

It would appear difficult to have made a worse choice. The merchant marine interested itself in figures quite other than those of displacement, which were perhaps the most significant for yachtsmen. It was not easy to determine a yacht's capacity from scantlings based on the requirements of the ordnance and victualling departments. The Excise, charged with tax collection, were interested in these and other facets of measurement only for the purpose of collecting revenue.

Furthermore there had never been a question of actually measuring physically the different dimensions of vessels. This would have been a long, costly and complicated operation since their forms and shapes are compound in all three dimensions. For a long time an arbitrary and approximate formula had been used which was enough for Customs officials to use in calculating the 'capacity' of a vessel under the law. This merely took into account the length along the keel and the beam—the depth (*not* draft) was taken as half the beam. This last measurement was therefore twice penalised in the formula. The designer G.L. Watson, in a study of the subject, marvelled that years and years passed before naval architects and builders realised that one could achieve a considerable rule advantage by reducing the beam to the profit of the other dimensions. Furthermore, sport was astern of commerce. In the 'good old days' British merchantmen had developed enormous draft and a reduced beam—a fact which probably explains the superiority of the American clippers, which were built on saner lines.

In 1828 other rules were put into force and it is from this point or thereabouts that organised yacht measurement may deem to have been launched. Apart from that there was nothing particularly noteworthy about these rules themselves which were mostly concerned with interdictions. This made for even more acerbic disputes which imposed themselves on the already heated arguments provoked by the original rules. It was thus that alterations to ballasting came to be forbidden. Writers of the day were not slow to inveigh against this practice which obliged an owner to sacrifice the interior accomodation of his yacht if he wanted results—lockers, furnishings, bunks all had to go to make way for pigs of ballast and the men who heaved them around. Equally, the setting of head sails on spars was banned. This must be considered as an attempt to limit the amount of sail carried down wind in spite of the fact that sail area was in no way measured under the rule. We read also that no member of the Royal Yacht Club could enter more than one boat in any one race. This was the counter-blow to a current practice—that of entering a light weather boat and a heavy weather one and sailing the one most likely to do best in the weather conditions of the day.

In the next year, 1829, the Royal Yacht Club attempted for the first time to separate competing yachts in terms of tonnage classifications. At the same time there was an effort to establish a handicap system whereby boats in different tonnage brackets could race against each other. The principal used was calculated on the *length* of the course in terms of distance, which is still the basis of handicap racing in the Mediterranean Sea. This, in its operational form, was the 'Tonnage Rule': It provided for four classes. Class I conceded a half mile to Class II, one and a quarter miles to Class III and two and a quarter miles to Class IV. It was a rough and ready method—which hardly ever gave a satisfactory result. Two years later the 'Tonnage Rule' became very much due for revision. This time Class I was to consist of the smallest yachts—that is those under 45 tons, and in this class the span was to be 5 tons. The largest boats were grouped in Class VI and there the tonnage span was 30. King George IV gave his official approval for these measures by indicating that from 1834 the King's Cup would be raced for under the new arrangements. The next important date was 1838, which saw the first of the Queen's Cups of the Victorian reign and another attempt to deal with handicapping. This time it was decided to use the factor of time in place of that of distance. Each difference of 10 tons rated 3 minutes and this was applied at

*ROYAL YACHT
SQUADRON
14 AUGUST 1844*

Mystery *approaches the buoy rolling heavily.. The yachts which have already rounded carry full sail. They were heavily built in those days. Besides which crews had not yet learned to ease their sheets off the wind....*

(Lithograph. G. Hawkins. Macpherson Collection.)

the start. This was less complicated than one might suppose, as it was often the case that yachts were started at anchor. This method is sometimes used in France and occasionally in England at the end of the season or on the occasion of a 'jolly' as a form of pursuit race. Competing craft leave in succession according to their handicap, the fastest being the last to leave. The basis of the system postulates then that all yachts should arrive at the finish at the same time—and the one that breaks the tapes first is the one to have been most skilfully handled. As it turned out this method was just as unsatisfactory as its predecessor—but it was a definite improvement in that *time* had been substituted for *distance*.

In 1841 there was yet another modification—for by now a fair method of handicapping had become the number one problem. Yachts started at the same time and there was an allowance of one second for each mile for each ton of measurement difference between competitors.

In 1843 the yachts were yet again reclassified, into cutters and schooners. The cutters were grouped into four divisions: 30 tons to under 50 tons, 50 tons to under 75, 75 tons to under 105 and 105 tons and above. The schooners were simply split into two divisions—140 tons and below, and above 140 tons. I don't need to remind you that there were few centreboard dinghies in those days. It was at this point that a new handicap system based on time, conceived by George Holland-Ackers, was put forward. Holland-Ackers was an active yachtsman. He owned the schooner *Dolphin* of 217 tons—and later the *Brilliant* and the *Rose Diamond*. The 'Ackers Rule' was a great improvement. To a certain extent 'rule making' had become an established occupation and legislators had come to stay in yacht racing. Ackers perhaps can justly be awarded the title of 'the first of the experts'. Before long, rules as such were doing more than simply determining handicaps. Inevitably they were to be responsible for the creation of classes built to the determining rule.

We come then to the end of the first half of the nineteenth century. The sport was still living in its heroic era, but already hints of the future were beginning to be seen. There were no less than sixteen active yacht clubs in England. There were a hundred vessels inscribed on the 'tablets' of the Royal Yacht Squadron*. The burgee of the Royal Thames Yacht Club was worn by 130 craft, and even the Royal Western Yacht Club mustered no less than eighty. And don't forget that we are talking about yachts which were, many of them, really small ships.

There was much going on between America and England in the last half of the nineteenth century. As it was destined perhaps, it really started with the meeting—or perhaps the clash—between the best that both countries could put forward in sailing vessels.

In 1851 when the *America*, a product of the luxuriant growth of 'Yachting Americana', came to take the measure of her 'elders' in the British Isles (and not without some misgivings) she met a veritable flotilla of yachts ready to repulse her challenge. How the *America* brought off a resounding victory over the finest flower of Britannia's yachts, how she took back to the United States a cup which dozens of yachts and millions of pounds have since sought to recapture—all that is a history in itself and need not be recounted here.

While doing their best, unsuccessfully, to avoid defeat, the British were certainly impressed by Yankee superiority and Yankee lines. A veritable fashion was established for cutting back the forefoot of yachts and making the waterline entries hollow and well drawn out.

To take contemporary accounts at their face value, the quarter century which followed was the apogee of the sailing yacht. It is difficult to disagree. This was the era of the Glory of Sail. The multitude, the size, and

*The 'Club' had become the 'Squadron' in 1833.

JULIA LEADS THE RACE (1853)

This cutter of 111 tons, built by Ratsey at Cowes, is seen beating the American sloop Sylvie *of 205 tons. The latter was built by George Steers, who was responsible for the illustrious* America. *She came to England to repeat the success of the older boat. She was thrashed by* Sylvie *in their first encounter and to such effect that her owner never appeared in a race again—or so it is said.*

(Lithograph. T.G. Dutton. Macpherson Collection.)

the beauty of the schooners and the great cutters which matched each other is legendary. Alas! few illustrations of this grand era have come down to us. The camera and the Bekens were yet to come on the scene, and we have to rely on the often crude prints of the time. But as you will see in this book, it is impossible to remain insensible to their charm.

The decade 1860 to 1870 saw the great days of the schooner. Over thirty of these magnificent vessels were racing regularly and there were many marvellous names to the roll-call—*Aline, Alarm, Titania, Gloriana, Cambria* and *Egeria*. After 1870 new names came to reinforce the fleet, but we need only recall *Livonia, Shamrock, Cetonia, Waterwitch,* and perhaps *Miranda*. During this same epoch the great cutters also embellished the scene. Before 1870 a 'census' reveals nearly thirty—and among that company were such 'pioneers' as *Arrow, Lulworth, Menai, Volante, Fiona,* and at will you can add ten or a dozen to that number, the most notable of which was the G.L. Watson *Vanduara,* the first hull to be all-steel built. The fleet of 40-tonners was by now firmly established on the Clyde—and the big yawls were beginning to make their appearance.

In spite of this, a few years later the sport was almost dead on its feet. It seemed as if it had killed itself. Naval architects and owners had gradually come to build deliberately to the faults in the rules and to exploit their weaknesses. The resulting type was a vessel of reduced beam and enormous draft. If their performance was hardly convincing, they got their own back when it came to totting up harbour and light dues and suchlike imposts!

In 1854, the 'Rule of 94' had been abandoned by the Revenue men and the merchant marine and had been replaced by a measurement of internal capacity, but the bad old ways which had produced an undesirable vessel remained in force for yachts. The builders discovered that it was possible to reduce the penalty on beam by increasing draft. They also found, when it came to ballast, that for the same nominal tonnage one could not only get a longer boat but one capable of carrying more canvas. Now it was that lead started to oust internal pig iron as ballast. Soon someone had the idea of fixing lead ballast on the outside of the vessel, in spite of the prophecies of doom from the traditionalists. Yachts became narrower and narrower with each succeeding design. The affair reached a point when Watson was driven to write that the whole thing approached Euclid's definition of a line—as having length but no thickness.

These were the salad days of the 'planks on edge'. *Irex* reduced the great racing cutters to the status of mere cruisers. *Miranda* with a mainsail the size of a cutter's behind her foresail sowed confusion among the schooners. *Annasona* and *Tara* were the cocks of the walk among the 'forties', *Clara* ruled the roost among the 'twenties'. But such vessels became more and more disagreeable. They lay down and sailed at incredible angles of heel. Their motion in a seaway was appallingly abrupt and brutal. The glamour died as owners became disenchanted with the general discomfort which attended such behaviour. Steam, which was becoming harnessable in terms of propulsive power, gained ground.

The need to repair this situation was only too evident. Ir was clear too that something effective had to be done about ending the confusion which reigned to a greater or lesser degree in yacht-racing everywhere. Each yacht club had its own measurement classifications as well as its own racing rules. This helped little except to add to the friction between competitors from different areas. Moreover it militated against any national or international uniformity.

It was not surprising therefore that in 1875 a number of British yachtsmen got together on their own initiative to form the Yacht Racing Association. Their proceedings were followed with great interest by a great number of people who put to sea for pleasure.

THE AMERICA AT COWES IN 1851

This is how she looked to those English sceptics, the yacht whose name for over a century has epitomised Anglo-American rivalry in sail. That America proved supreme was mainly due to her sails—their cut, their few numbers and their great size. She was however almost equally distinguished by her finer lines and her hollow entry. Paradoxically, and for lack of adversaries, America only won one race in English waters—and owes her fame to the struggles of other and later vessels.

The object of the promoters—Count Edmond Bathyazy, Captain Hughes and the naval architect Dixon Kemp —was simply to systematize yacht-racing. This step was not particularly revolutionary since the Y.R.A. measurement rule was by all the evidence a direct heir of the old formula. But the great advantage was that it was at least to be administered by a national authority.

The succeeding year inevitably saw the first modifications to the rule, but from now on clubs were to print on their race programmes the magic words 'under the rules of the Y.R.A.' This did not automatically lessen the number of Homeric bouts between owners and between crews, but it was a most important move in the right direction.

By 1881 the Y.R.A. had mustered sufficient authority to enable the Association to adopt a new measurement rule with the certitude that no one would question or contest its provisions. The rule which read:

$$\frac{(L+B)^2 \times B}{1730}$$

was intended to reduce the penalty on beam which was the feature of the 'Rule of 94'.

In practice, the new formula was only more lenient on beam up to a point where the yacht's length equalled $5\frac{1}{4}$ times the beam. Above this, beam was in fact *more* heavily penalised. It had been hoped that builders would be encouraged to build boats with bigger beam to secure advantage of the new rule. But the benefit of this factor was nowhere near large enough to overcome the current trend, which was to go all out for length at any price and to ignore the virtues of a reasonable amount of beam. Boats became even more herring-gutted—to such an extent that by 1886 practically everyone was calling for a *radical* revision of rule, not just modifications here and there. In the autumn a committee of the Y.R.A., after collecting

and sifting the advice of diverse experts, decided to adopt a rule proposed by Dixon Kemp based solely on waterline length and sail area. Beam and draft played no part in the Dixon Kemp formula. The effect was to leave experimentation in beam wide open. Centreboards were permitted and the pessimists were quick to assert that the pass had been sold to all sorts and shapes of 'saucers and other fantasies', but as it turned out, the almost excessive circumspection of builders meant that they only slowly and timidly explored the opportunities offered to them.

The new rule read:

$$\frac{Length \times Sail\ Area}{6000} = Rating$$

The first notable yacht to appear under this writ was the G. L. Watson designed *Thistle*—conceived for American waters and an assault on the America's Cup. In 1889, however, Alfred Payne built the $2\frac{1}{2}$ Rater *Humming Bird* which exploited beam, and she easily disposed of the earlier, narrower champions in the class. But she was only one small boat. For obvious reasons, one sees that 'daring' experiments like this were preferably executed in the field of the small boat. In 1890 the famous *Iverna* was built, and nothing much more of importance happened before 1893. In that year it was once more a Royal initiative which gave a new impulse to the scene. The Prince of Wales ordered *Britannia* from Watson. The same year saw *Navahoe, Vigilant, Colonia, Jubilee* and *Pilgrim*.

Britannia's subsequent career pleads eloquently for the virtue of this measurement rule, but at the time she was by no means considered a 'non pareil'. She was particularly criticised for setting a fashion for over-beamy boats, drawing too much water and of insufficient displacement (she was 23 feet on the beam and drew 15 feet 3 inches)! Another point of contention was that in the effort to reduce wetted surface, keels started to become more and more cut away both

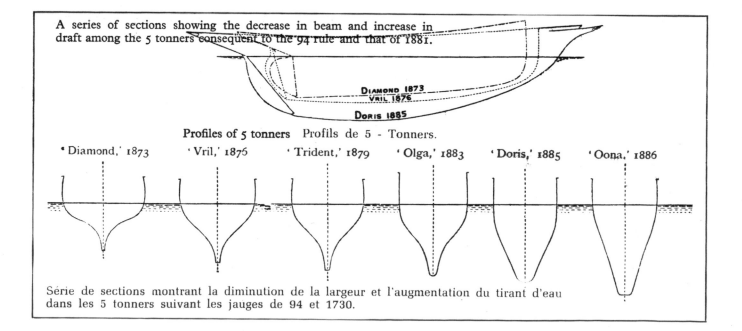

A series of sections showing the decrease in beam and increase in draft among the 5 tonners consequent to the 94 rule and that of 1881.

Diamond 1873
Vril 1876
Doris 1885

Profiles of 5 tonners   Profils de 5 - Tonners.

'Diamond,' 1873   'Vril,' 1876   'Trident,' 1879   'Olga,' 1883   'Doris,' 1885   'Oona,' 1886

Série de sections montrant la diminution de la largeur et l'augmentation du tirant d'eau dans les 5 tonners suivant les jauges de 94 et 1730.

forward and aft. Designs nevertheless went forward on these lines and soon critics were describing them as 'costly to build, costly to operate, with neither headroom nor space below decks, and which would have broken up at the first occasion if they hadn't been so well constructed'. We can call this an exaggerated judgement in view of *Britannia*'s long career. However, if her size and her cost and the limitation of materials in those days were a brake to carrying things to excess at her level, the same could not be said for yachts in the smaller classes! Thus it came about in 1891 that a group of the foremost naval architects wrote a long letter to the Y.R.A., inviting them to modify the rule with a view to producing yachts which were more sensibly designed and more solidly constructed. Needless to say these exhortations were hardly listened to—which merely proves that there's nothing new under the sun.

For all that, a new formula was put up in 1896. Rating was now to be discovered by the following mathematics:

Length + Beam + ¾ immersed Girth at 0.6 of the waterline length from the stem + ½ √Sail Area and all divided by 2
= Rating

This one does not appear to have been very convincing and four years later, in 1900, yet another formula was adopted. This was destined to encourage yachts of fuller body.

It read as follows:

$$\frac{\text{Length} + \text{Beam} + \frac{3}{4}\,G + 4d + \frac{1}{2}\,\sqrt{\text{Sail Area}}}{2 \cdot 1} = \text{Rating}$$

'G' was the girth measurement obtained from a chain *stretched* from gunwhale to gunwhale at the previous girth station *after* deducting twice the freeboard at this particular point. 'd' was a new element and represented the difference between girth as measured by the tight chain and the actual distance around the hull section at the measurement station. The effect was to introduce a heavy penalty for boats with hollowed out sections below waterline. This penalty was of course at maximum in the case of fin-and-bulb keelers. This formula is credited to Alfred Benyon of Copenhagen. It seems to have been in use for some little time in Germany and Denmark before its introduction into English waters.

In 1906 there took place an event of exceptional significance. The Yacht Racing Association succeeded in convening an international conference which secured the support of all European nations interested in the sport. At this gathering a uniform system of measurement was agreed upon. As if this wasn't enough—one must remember that international conferences were in their infancy—the conference achieved agreement on the future building of racing yachts to common tables of scantlings for the various designated classes. Both steps were of the greatest importance and led to the birth of the International Yacht Racing Union. It was all the more regrettable therefore that the United States should have refused to play a part at the conference, preferring to adopt her own measurement rules and procedures. This fine example of the isolationist syndrome of America inevitably led to the development of an entirely different type of yacht.

A contemporary commentator wrote acidly: 'This attitude gave true international racing as much chance for the future as it had had in the past.' The schism is now sixty years old and is celebrated by one half of the world racing at sea under the rules of the Cruising Club of America and the other half under the writ of the Royal Ocean Racing Club.

The new international rule propounded by the 1906 conference had as its principal aims the encouragement of reasonable interior accommodations, the blocking of the tendency to excessive flair forward and the

CAMBRIA

The paintings and watercolours of the middle of the nineteenth century doubtless give a more exact image of the yachts of the day than the very first photographic prints. After having beating the American yacht Sappho *at Cowes and* Dauntless *across the Atlantic,* Cambria *was destined, in her role as challenger for the America's Cup, to play a less glorious part than these victories forecast for her. Defeated out of hand by the New York Yacht Club defence,* Cambria *was next beaten by an improved* Sappho. *After that, she lived out a long career as a coaster among the Antilles.*

(Lithograph. T.G. Dutton. T.H. Parker Collection.)

reduction of the long overhangs which were making their appearance. Sail area itself was more lightly 'taxed' and there was a premium placed on freeboard —all rather like a present day Budget speech. The designated classes were fixed at 5, 6, 7, 8, 10, 12, 15, 19, and 23 Metres and above. Handicaps on time were to be abolished and yachts were to race boat-for-boat in the appropriate categories. There was to be no concession for inferiority in rigging plans except only in the case of the largest class. This was a real revolution—which was successful up to a point. The thought behind it is today manifested in the conception of the Ton Cups.

To return to those times, the 52-footers, those yachts tating at 52 feet, were granted one further season's existence. *Britomart, Moyana* and *Sonya* were among rhese and happily enough the old 52-footers were near enough to the new 15 Metre international rule. Two new 15 Metres were immediately laid down, one from Mylne and the other from Fife. These new yachts were admitted with handicap to the 52-footer class for the extra year. Two new 23 Metres were also placed on order—one for Sir James Bender designed by Charles E. Nicholson, and the second by William Fife for M. B. Kennedy. The new rule may therefore be said to have got off to an excellent start. It was to last for many years and produce many wonderful racing yachts. The last of the line are the lovely 12 Metres, beautiful thoroughbreds who to this day dispute the America's Cup. But historically, as you will now see, greater tribute should perhaps be paid to the 6 Metres—modified and improved over fifty years—which provided competition of the highest order for so many years and thereby testified to the excellence of the 1906 international rule.

ROYAL THAMES YACHT CLUB RACE FROM THE NORE TO DOVER IN 1874

Cetonia, Gwendolen *and Florinda* have rounded the Goodwins lightship. Kriemhilda, *who was to win the race, is still astern with Egeria. In a few years, we are to see the first marine photographs and among them those of both* Egeria *and* Cetonia. *Photographs can seldom call up the tempests that the artists saw in the pictures they painted.*

(Lithograph. Rickett. Johnson Collection.)

VIEW OF DOVER IN 1860

In those days ships put to sea when the wind was favourable, and there were no power towing-boats in the ports and harbours. The horse and the sailing vessel were still the swiftest forms of transport. Certain yacht owners amused themselves by writing letters to Cherbourg from Cowes and sailing over to await their arrival. The world was different then—but that was how it looked a hundred years ago.

(Aquatint. Himely. Macpherson Collection.)

A Bermudan Schooner - 1834
(J. Lynn)

As the name indicates, it was in the waters of Bermuda that our modern rig first made its appearance. (That said, if the coast depicted here is a part of Bermuda then this writer too is a blackamoor. However, this 'Bermudan Schooner' may have been on a visit? The astonishing thing is the modern appearance of the rig - and she must be 130 years old or more. The spread of the base of the sailplan gives nothing away to some modern ocean cruisers, while the cut of those loose-footed sails aft of the masts, as well as of the headsail, are perfect. For all that the rigging looks on the light side!

The Dolphin - 1837

(Coloured Lithograph.
T. G. Dutton after N. M. Condy)

This schooner of 217 tons is notable for having been owned by G. Holland-Ackers, to whom a number of references are made in these pages. He introduced in particular the idea of corrected time handicapping into the Royal Yacht Squadron. Note the square topsails and the foresail brailed up to the mast after the fashion of the Thames barges.

FISHING FLEET IN

THIS is an historic photograph of exceptional quality. The cold majesty of the sea and the sky sets off the stark silhouettes which pass to and fro, bringing in the harvest of the sea for Victorian dining-rooms. One can almost feel the calloused hands of the crew on the rough trawl-lines and the stiff canvas. But this was of the race of men which crewed the great cutters you will find in this book. In a sense they had no nationality. They were sailors and belonged to the sea. In 1889, the year before this photograph, the Earl of Dunraven built his first Valkyrie, a 77 Rater, at Southampton. He won 23 cups in 33 starts, but was second to Yarana with 31 cups during the season. In the same year as the photograph, the negotiations between Dunraven and the New York Yacht Club for a challenge for the America's Cup broke down on the Royal Yacht Squadron's refusal to be bound to adhere to

THE NORTH SEA

the new 1887 rules in the case of a British victory. So Valkyrie stayed home in British waters under Skipper Diaper—and finished at the bottom of the fleet. The previous challenger, Thistle—later the Kaiser's yacht Meteor—led the fleet with 22 trophies, and Iverna was next with 20. A year later Iverna notched 22 victories to Valkyrie's 15.

The Earl of Dunraven, who was to play a major rôle on the yacht racing stage, was born in 1841. In 1887, at the age of 46, when sailing aboard Mr. John Jameson's Irex he became bitten with the bug and began his career among the giants of yachting.

1887 saw the introduction in the Sail Area Rule (Length × Sail Area - 6000 ÷ Rating). The first important boat to be built to the rule was Thistle, a 139 Rater, who was to be beaten in 'the Cup' races by the American, Volunteer.

$\mathcal{E}$GERIA must have been amongst the most successful of the 'old' racing schooners. She logged a magnificent history of prize wins for over a decade from 1865 when she was built into the late 1870's. Her owner throughout these years was Mr. J. Mulholland, who later became Lord Dunleath.

Time telescopes at this distance and the big yachts call to mind Watson and Fife, but Egeria was designed and built by Wanhill at Poole. Even at the time she was built she was spoken of as a schooner of great length—she was 72 feet long on her keel. She won the Royal Yacht Squadron Queen's Cup in 1865 and the adjective applied to her was that of 'handsome'. She and Blue Bell headed the schooners in the succeeding year. To give you an idea of the performance these vessels were capable of reaching, Blue Bell in a strong W.S.W. wind raced round the Isle of Wight in 5 hours 45 minutes. Egeria was again successful in 1867. In 1868 she was second only to the new schooner of 108 Tons T.M., the Ratsey built Cambria. Egeria again headed the schooners in 1869. In 1870 the first attempt to recover the America's Cup was made and it was Cambria who sailed against sixteen American yachts (to offset this numerical preponderance she was allowed to choose her starting berth—the yachts were anchored at the gun—and although opting for the weather pitch this became the leeward one owing to a wind shift). In any event, Cambria this year had little claim to being the best of the British schooners. She was beaten 6 out of 7 by Egeria and if anything the 95 ton Flying Cloud had the most successes by a few races over Egeria. 1871 saw the appearance of Mr. Ashbury's Ratsey 265 tonner Livonia, the next Cup challenger. Egeria beat her twice and proved the best schooner of the season, finishing just ahead of Flying Cloud on aggregate.

This astonishing history goes on in the same style. In 1872 Egeria was still spoken of and written about as the fastest schooner afloat. In 1873 she was second to an old rival Pantomine. In 1874 she was second to the new Ratsey Cetonia. In 1875 when the rule was changed from the Royal Thames to the Yacht Racing Association rule she was still scoring. She was successful in 1876 although five of the other schooners did not race. The heyday of the schooner was now in full decline and in 1877 this famous vessel was absent from the regatta programmes for the first time in twelve years. She was out again in 1878 but the schooner was now completely eclipsed by the yawl.

As the photograph shows she was undoubtedly a fine ship. Nevertheless a tremendous amount of credit is owed to Mr. Mulholland who built her and raced her throughout her fabulous career. (P. 20-21).

$\mathcal{W}$HITE SLAVE was quite a strange boat altogether apart from the 'lugger rig' she is sporting in the photograph, which incidentally was taken in 1890. She was a 40 Rater, though not a successful one, and built rather mysteriously in 1890 by a G. Gausden at Eastbourne, about whom little or nothing is known. Her owner Mr. F.W. Leybourne Popham is associated in the records with the design of White Slave. The name of Mr. William Fife, jnr., also appears, though anything less like one's concept of a Fife yacht is difficult to picture.

In 1894 she was rigged as a cutter and owned by a Mr. William Walter Maclellan—so one seems to be safe in saying that the 'lugger rig' does not appear to have been a successful racing rig.

Egeria: Length T. M. 98.4 ft. Length W. L. 93.8 ft. Breadth 19.2 ft. Depth 18.1 ft.

White Slave: Length T.M. 63.0 ft. Length W.L. 60.0 ft. Breadth 14.0ft. Depth 10.0 ft. Tons T.M. 51.

*B*LOODHOUND was one of the most famous yachts of her day —exactly as is her namesake, owned by Her Majesty Queen Elizabeth II, to-day. She was the work of William Fife, jnr., and was built at his yard in 1874 for the Marquis of Ailsa. She represents the apogee of the old straight-stemmed cutter. She was a '40 tonner' under the Royal Thames Yacht Club rule then in use:

$$\frac{L—B \times (B \times \frac{1}{2}B)}{94}$$

L being length between perpendiculars and B the measured Beam. A form of Thames Tonnage —Thames Measurement—exists as a bit of an anachronism to-day.

Bloodhound started winning prizes almost from the day of her launch. Norman and Britannia were the head boats with 9 first prizes each, but Bloodhound was not far behind with 7. In 1875 she was the crack '40 tonner'. She was most solidly built and went on winning prizes with impressive regularity. In six seasons she collected 72 before passing into the hands of Thomas Dunlop, who brought in another 28 between 1902 and 1906.

After Bloodhound the Marquis of Ailsa built first the famous Foxhound, and then Sleuthhound. This photograph was taken in August 1913 when Bloodhound was a young forty years old.

Bloodhound: Length T.M. 62.0 ft. Breadth 12.3 ft. Depth 7.8 ft. Tons T.M. 40.

*J*ULLANAR, built in 1875 near Maldon on the Blackwater, has the reputation of having been something of a design breakthrough. In truth she probably represented a breakaway from the influence, felt in the first half of the century, of the smaller naval vessels of the time. She was designed by E. H. Bentall and J. Hervey and built by Bentall, who was an agricultural implement maker!—a calling probably not much influenced by the line of thought then current in the design of naval vessels. She was an undoubted departure from existing types—and writers some thirty years later speak of her appearance creating a mild sensation. Certainly she was distinguished by an immersed counter ending in a 'canoe stern' and a vertical rudder post, but neither of these features seems likely to have produced anything resembling a breakthrough on its own. A more likely reason for her success is to be found in a finer entry and a cleaner run than her sisters and rivals. These are suggested in the way in which she is sailing in the photograph. Agricultural implement maker or not, the boat Bentall designed and built could plough the waves all right since in 1877, when she first appeared in the racing list, she proved the best of the yawls—a rig which was then becoming fashionable. In 1878 the yawls were a strong class and Jullanar's performance of the previous season had excited interest. She further enhanced her reputation by not only heading the yawls but achieving the best record of any yacht that year. She was at her best in hard winds but was to be reckoned with in almost all conditions. Although our eyes can see little to grumble about in this handsome vessel, anxious and doubtless jealous glances judged her as surpassing everything afloat for ugliness in those days!

*T*HE dimensions of BRITANNIA are elsewhere in this book. The interest of this photograph is that it shows what it took to hoist Britannia's jackyard topsail and to set her main. In the picture there are 25 hands heaving away—my hearties ho! There is one at the mainmast cap, another up the ratlines near the futtocks, twelve on the foredeck on the tail of the halyard—and eight who have swarmed up the ratlines to put their weight on the halyard! Tough stuff.
On one occasion the Prince of Wales (later King Edward VII) was leaning over the main hatch, smoking a cigar and watching the crew hauling the mainsail aloft. Through mistiming or misjudgement the weight of the sail overcame the weight of the crew and, 'falling on the Prince's head and shoulders, knocked him unconscious'. Those were the days! (P. 28.)

Jullanar: Length T.M. 90.8 ft. Breadth 16.6 ft. Depth 13.1 ft. Tons T.M. 126.

T HIS is an old photograph indeed. It was taken at Gosport in 1882. LYRA herself was designed and built by Camper & Nicholson in 1876. In the photograph her crew is running aloft on the ratlines in the main rigging in order to hang their weight on the fall of the main halyards—throat and peak—so as to get the mainsail hoisted! Observe too the men aloft aboard the 'man-o'-war'!

Five years after the photograph was taken Lyra was lengthened by 36 feet!—an engine room

was installed, and she was converted to a steamer. The engine was an interesting piece of ironmongery. It was made by W.B. Thomson & Co. and was an inverted 3 cylinder. One cylinder of 13ins. diameter, one of 19ins. and one of 33ins! Stroke was 24ins. and the whole thing operated at 150 p.s.i. boiler pressure. An interesting vessel—and a most interesting photograph.

Lyra: Length T.M. 169.0 ft. Breadth 25.6 ft. Depth 14.1 ft. Tons T.M. 500.

Mystery and Blue Bell racing in 1843
(Coloured Lithograph.
E. G. Dutton after N. M. Condy)

Apparently a match race on the Thames between owners could be an important enough affair to be recorded for posterity, even when it concerned small yachts (these two are 25 tonners). The picture shows the decisive moment of the match. Blue Bell, the farthest from the artist's easel, has gone aground on False Point and Mystery, finding a passage between her opponent and the Thames shore, escapes and goes on to win.

The America at Cowes in 1851

(Colour Lithograph.
T. G. Dutton after Oswald W. Brierly)

Here she is! The American schooner is represented crossing the finishing line at the end of the race for a cup presented by the Royal Yacht Squadron which was to make her famous around the world. The crew affect a nonchalance which was far from usual in those days.

$\mathcal{A}$ classic photograph of the vintage of 1887! Great black-hulled, sturdy boats they were in those days—and built like churches to the glory of God and to last for more than one generation! They had great ferocious bowsprits made from full grown trees. Their stems were hard, uncompromising, upright pillars of oak. Their topsides were as thick as a man's arm and ringed around with bulwarks like battlements.

The third boat from the left is looking for room to lower her spinnaker boom to full stretch and the clew of the spinnaker has already been run out a fifth of the way along the spar. Activity on the decks of these veterans is intense for this is a start at close quarters and these mastodons were not the most manœuvrable of 'racing machines'. (P. 30-31)

$\mathcal{T}$HE building of SLEUTHHOUND by Fife at Fairlie to a design by William Fife jnr. for the Marquis of Ailsa marked the last of the development of the old straightstemmed '40 tonners', who traced their ancestry directly back to the navy, the preventive service and the pilots—the protectors and the policemen of the fishermen around the coasts. Sleuthhound was the third of the Marquis's 'hounds'. Preceding her were first Foxhound and then Bloodhound. She was built in 1881 and there were two other new '40 tonners' that year, the others being another Fife yacht Annasona and a G. L. Watson design, May. All three were of narrower beam and greater displacement than say Norman, the most successful of the existing vintage at the time. All three were much faster vessels. Annasona proved the best of the new bunch and Sleuthhound rather disappointing—but Annasona had a particularly fine helmsman in O'Neil.

1882 saw the introduction of the new Y.R.A. Tonnage Rule—which as a matter of fact was no better than the rule it replaced. Annasona was still the crack boat in the class in this year with Sleuthhound second. In 1883 Annasona was missing O'Neil at the helm and was displaced by May. Sleuthhound was bottom of the league.

In 1887 the Tonnage Rule was dropped in favour of a new Sail Area Rule. However that's beside the point. In this year the Royal Thames Y.C. presented a handsome prize (1,000 guineas in 1887 would be worth £7,000 today?) for a race round Great Britain and Ireland to commemorate Queen Victoria's jubilee. The sailing distance was 1,600 sea miles and it lasted over 14 days. Sleuthhound came second to Genesta!

The photograph amuses with the headgear showing above the bulwarks in the stern sheets. One appears to be a 'wide-awake' and the other a 'Billy-cock' or bowler.

Sleuthhound: Length T.M. 68.45 ft.   Length W.L. 64.07 ft.   Breadth 9.6 ft.   Depth 9.6 ft.   Tons T.M. 45.

THIS photograph misleads. We have been so used to the larger vessels of the day that ULERIN takes our eye immediately as being yet another of those superb and colossal cutters which graced the great days of yachting. But this is not the case. Ulerin was of the '10-ton' class and as you see from the statistics she was only just over 40 feet on the waterline and by comparison a smallish boat at that time. She was designed by G. L. Watson and built by W. Shute at Southampton in 1884.

In that year there were two new '10-tonners'—Ulerin built for E. H. Hamilton and the W. Fife snr. designed Marguerite for J. C. Macindoe. Racing between these two in the North was particularly closely contested. Although Ulerin came out with far the best prize record, each race had to be fought all round the course and the margins of victory were nearly always narrow and exciting. When Ulerin came south she defeated the Solent champion Buttercup. In all she won 27 prizes by the end of the season, most of them first flags, in spite of not being in racing commission until the Mersey regattas quite late on in the season.

Ulerin had a particularly successful season in the succeeding year, 1885. She had been bought by Sir Edgar Vincent and her main rival in the South was Queen Mab, a new Watson yacht for Mr. T. S. C. West. At first she made a poorish showing, but a change of skipper worked wonders and she came out superior to the new boat. After this she went north to renew her rivalry with Marguerite. The latter had been improved to the tune of winning 7 out of the 13 races they sailed.

Still Ulerin was a most successful yacht and—as the photo shows—one with a handsome air to her as well as a handsome performance to go with it.

AMPHITRITE was a Camper & Nicholson schooner built for Colonel A.D. MacGregor in 1887. She rated 13.163 and sailed in the 1890's. In the early half of this decade the cruisers were out in great force. The photograph depicts the last of that maritime age which was born from the small naval ships of the era of Trafalgar and the Nile. The clipper bow dates the scene when one remembers that not many years before this shot was taken Watson was still hesitating to give his designs what was called a 'spoon bow'—not the most graceful sounding term for a feature that is attractive to our eyes. Note also the vertical cloths in the mainsail, which were later to be sewn up horizontally.

CETONIA, reaching up astern, was built in 1873 for Mr. W. Turner and was later acquired by Sir Edward Guinness (later to become Lord Iveagh). She was built by M. Ratsey at Cowes—and Ratseys were boat builders then! She rated 156.54 ft. and set some 9,300 sq.ft. of canvas. Cetonia was really a very great ship. She cannot be said to have been an outstanding racing boat. Lord Iveagh replaced her with a famous namesake who carried that name for thirty-five years. (P. 38-39.)

Ulerin: Length T.M. 43.2 ft. Length W.L. 41.5 ft. Breadth 7.2 ft. Depth 7.0 ft. Tons T.M. 10.

Amphitrite: Length T.M. 100.2 ft. Length W.L. 93.82 ft. Breadth 12.3 ft. Depth 12.3 ft. Tons T.M. 161.

DURING the winter preceeding the season of 1889 there had been rumours of an eighth challenge for the America's Cup following Thistle's unsuccessful match with Volunteer. The Earl of Dunraven had been casting his eyes in this direction and had been negotiating with the New York Yacht Club. To this end also, he went to G. L. Watson for a challenger and built her at Fay's yard in Southampton. She was named VALKYRIE and rated 77·42.

Dunraven's negotiations broke down however. After the secrecy that had surrounded Thistle's dimensions and the fact that a wrong measurement had been declared by the challenger, the Americans instituted a new Deed of Gift. Among provisions that the British found irksome was the requirement that a challenger's dimensions must be declared ten months before the event.

Valkyrie: Length B.P. 85.0 ft. Length W.L. 69.26 ft. Breadth 15.9 ft. Depth 11.6 ft. Tons T.M. 94.

When it came to the Valkyrie challenge the New York Y.C. sought assurances that in the event of a British victory these new terms would be adhered to. This the Royal Yacht Squadron refused. The challenge therefore never took place and it was only in 1892 that a compromise was reached requiring only the waterline length to be revealed.

Nevertheless all this toing-and-froing focused attention on Valkyrie's performance during the season—after all she might have been across the Atlantic fighting the 'damn Yankees'. Valkyrie proved very difficult to beat in moderate weather. She could not however stay with Yarana in the light stuff. This pattern repeated itself in the following year. When the time came to build Valkyrie II for the 1893 Cup series, Valkyrie passed first into Austrian and then into Sicilian ownership.

The photograph shows her at speed in slightly less than her preferred weight of wind—but striding along nevertheless. It is interesting to note the crewman aloft at the heel of the main topmast.

VALKYRIE II was the Earl of Dunraven's second weapon of assault on American yacht racing supremacy as expressed by the America's Cup and its seemingly permanent domicile in the New York Yacht Club. Like her earlier namesake she was a Watson design but this time it was Henderson's on Clydeside who were the builders and not Fay's at Southampton. Valkyrie fought the 1893 races against Vigilant. In the first event in light weather Valkyrie lead by 26 minutes at the first mark but the race became void at the expiry of the time limit. The race was re-run. Once again Valkyrie led in the early stages but was caught and passed when the breeze freshened.

The second race was held over the triangular course brought in under the new 'rules' and the off-wind legs appeared to favour the defence. The third race in strong winds was quite definitely going Valkyrie's way and she led at the weather mark by two minutes. But on the run she blew out her spinnaker and thereafter was defeated by the seamanship aboard Vigilant. The defender's crew succeeded in shaking out the reef in the mainsail in half a gale and brought her storming through. That was naturally that, in the best of five. But Valkyrie II had conducted herself with distinction. She could have won both the first and the third races with just a bit more luck.

In British waters Valkyrie and Britannia confronted each other frequently and the contests were very closely fought. In fact so closely fought were they that these protagonists were often in collision. There was a memorable three boat collision on one particular Dover-Boulogne race, when the crew of Valkyrie extricated themselves from a spectacular involvement by cutting away Britannia's bowsprit!

This photograph shows Valkyrie racing against the new Herreshoff designed and built NAVAHOE. Valkyrie has had the better of this episode in a Royal London Yacht Club regatta, breaking out her jib first and forcing her way through Navahoe's lee.

In 1894 Valkyrie's Cup rival Vigilant sailed across the Atlantic to race in British waters. It was on the occasion of their first encounter on the Clyde—an event awaited with much interest —that Valkyrie was rammed and sunk by Satanita in a tragedy we describe in more detail elsewhere. Britannia was left to defeat Vigilant, in the first of a tremendous series of races between these two boats. Navahoe's measurements are given on page 59. (P. 42-43.)

Valkyrie II: Length B.P. 97.8 ft. Length W.L. 86.8 ft. Breadth 21.7 ft. Depth 12.95 ft. Tons T.M. 191.

$\mathcal{A}$LFONSO XIII, King of Spain, and his uncle, King Edward VII, aboard Britannia.

The Emperor Wilhelm II of Germany at Cowes. Before seeking military glory in tragic circumstances and with even more tragic consequences, and ambitious to make Germany or Prussia—whichever you will—a mighty naval power, the Hohenzollern went to great lengths to become a yachtsman of the first rank. His insistence on precedence and protocol and his taste for uniform made even stiff-lipped Englishmen smile. He reacted strongly to the more conservative elements in the Royal Yacht Squadron—perhaps they reacted that way to him—but he did get in perhaps one of the best cracks of the era. Someone asked the whereabouts of King Edward VII

A SPORT
OF KINGS

—he was out aboard Sir Thomas Lipton's yacht—and it was the Kaiser who said, 'My cousin is sailing with his grocer.' He put up numerous cups and trophies, with a varying amount of success. On one evening following a regatta, King George V of Britain perceived that the Gold Cup which had just been presented to him was merely plated, so he placed it conveniently to foot and 'accidentally' kicked it overboard. Another Gold Cup, awarded for a transatlantic race, found its way to the United States and when America entered the first World War it was symbolically melted down as a contribution to the war effort. But there again it was a case of 'all that glisters is not gold'. Beneath a gold skin the cup was found to be of very ordinary alloy. . . .

SATANITA was also of the vintage year of 1893. She was building in Southampton at the same time that Valkyrie II and Britannia were coming into being on Clydeside. These three together with Calluna and the older Iverna formed the Big Five of that year. Although she was beaten by both the Watson designs (Britannia first by 3 seconds from Valkyrie in the Royal Thames Nore to Dover match) she gave promise of her performance to come by covering the 13¾ miles from the Tongue Lightship to North Sandhead in just over one hour. Perhaps it was her destiny to be a wayward vessel—anyhow she was soon modified by cutting three feet off her mast and the shipping of additional lead. Her performance improved but on the Clyde she was shortly to be involved in misfortune when her gaff tangled in Valkyrie's topmast shrouds and in a later race she burst her bobstay and broke her bowsprit. She was a hard breeze boat and her speed with her sheets freed was remarkable. In the Cowes Town Cup of that year she sailed the 48 miles course in 3 hours 40 minutes and 50 seconds—13 knots—but truth to tell this design of Soper's was not quite the equal of Watson's Britannia.

For the start of 1894 her sail area was increased, perhaps to put her on terms with her rival. But it was this year that the fatal incident with Valkyrie II occurred on the Clyde. Contemporary accounts give the story as follows. The race was one for amateur helmsmen and a good strong wind was blowing at the time. Satanita was standing up the Holy Loch on starboard and Valkyrie was coming into the line on port tack. The anchorage was crowded with yachts and from this jungle there appeared a small boat across Satanita's bow. Her helmsman bore away to avoid this craft only to find the target doing the same thing. Satanita was then luffed to avoid the intruder and then her helm was put up to avoid Valkyrie. She failed to respond in time: 100 feet on the waterline and travelling fast?—it's not surprising. She took Valkyrie head-on just abaft the mast and cut her down to the waterline. Valkyrie staggered against the steam-yacht Hebe and a crewman who tried to scramble aboard the steamer was fatally injured. She then fell foul of the steam-yacht Vanduara and her topmast came down. After drifting clear she sank head foremost in 14 fathoms. It must have been a shattering spectacle. Satanita subsequently had her sail area reduced and finished the season with 6 prizes against Britannia's 31. In 1895 the topic was all a new Watson designed Valkyrie III to challenge for the America's Cup and the defenders laid down the appropriately named Defender. Satanita did not fit out. In 1896 after only nine years the Yacht Racing Association changed the Sail Area Rule to a new Linear Rating Rule.

Satanita is last mentioned racing in 1906, rigged as a yawl with 10,300 sq.ft. of canvas—her Linear Rating then being 101·54—when at Cowes she won both the King's Cup and the German Emperor's Cup—so after thirteen years she was still a formidable weapon on her day. She was bought in 1897 by Sir Maurice Fitzgerald, a noted horse racing man, and performed successfully on the Riviera. In the autumn of 1898 she made a passage in front of a northeast gale from Land's End to Valencia (Ireland), a distance of nearly 300 miles, in exactly 20 hours—just short of 15 knots average. It was in this year that she was altered to a yawl from her cutter rig. In 1909 she was sold to an Italian buyer.

Satanita: Length B.P. 127.1 ft. Length W.L. 102.1 ft. Breadth 23.7 ft. Depth 12.4 ft. Tons T.M. 400.

*A*RIADNE was almost more of a ship than a yacht! She was 380 tons T.M., and Camper and Nicholson designed and built her in 1874. Twenty-three years later she was the largest yacht to take part in the 310 mile race from Dover to Heligoland for the Emperor's Diamond Jubilee Cup.

We note here the helmsman and one other solitary figure in state aft and the crew grouped forward of the foremast. They knew their places in those days! Observe too the 'lugger type' topsails, which were to develop into the more efficient jack-yard. They in turn gave way of course to the full Bermudan mainsail. The overlapping forestaysail is also interesting. It rather strange for this type of sail to have taken so many years to reappear as a 'genoa'. Again it is quite clear that with big sail areas and a big crew to work them, really big boats could be made to move —look at the bone in Ariadne's teeth. (P. 48-49.)

*T*HESE are the 40 Raters of the 1890's. In 1892 three new '40's' were built of which the A. E. Payne designed CORSAIR was one. The other two were the G. L. Watson Queen Mab and Varuna. Queen Mab was a centreboarder but sailed just as well without it and so discarded it. She was also the most successful, but Corsair is spoken of as being extremely well designed with a powerful midsection. She was the next most prize-laden yacht and ran Queen Mab closely enough on occasions. In 1893 Queen Mab was sold to America and Admiral the Hon. Victor Montagu replaced Corsair with Vendetta. The new Fife designed LAIS was ready early in the season and headed the prize list with 29 prizes in 39 starts. So here are two of the three most successful '40's' battling it out in threatening conditions—much as they did all that year. (P. 50-51.)

*T*HE splendid American NAVAHOE, designed by Herreshoff, leads the fleet of the 'first rate' cutters in 1893. This was of course one of the most successful years of big class racing with Britannia, Bona, Navahoe, Satanita, Calluna and Iverna all competing. The last three named are all astern of Navahoe in the picture. Perhaps the other two have already passed on their way? Or perhaps Britannia has, for one may descry another 'big one' trailing astern which might be Bona, who was at her best in light winds. Navahoe has a much bigger, much longer-hoist jib-topsail set. One can see the amount of stretch and sag that this has produced in the topmast forestay, which makes it difficult to sheet the sail in hard. For all that she is tramping along. There is a fine smother of white water along her lee rail and her wake stretches almost as far back as Satanita's stem as she ploughs along next astern. Navahoe's measurements are given on page 59.

VALKYRIE
CALLUNA
IVERNA

*T*HE year 1893 was one of the most exceptional in yachting history. It was marked by the appearance of the then Prince of Wales (later King Edward VII) as the owner of a new yacht of 151 Rating—Britannia. In the autumn of the previous year the Earl of Dunraven commissioned the firm of G. L. Watson to design a new challenger for the America's Cup to be named VALKYRIE II. The Prince of Wales followed his lead and the yachts were built side-by-side at the yard of D. & W. Henderson at Partick on the Clyde. At the same time J. G. Fay & Son at Southampton, who in 1890 had built IVERNA for Mr. John Jameson, were building Satanita to design of J. M. Soper for Mr. A. D. Clarke.

These notable additions to the fleet of the great cutters—stimulated by the new Dunraven challenger—caused great excitement everywhere. A Clyde syndicate was hastily formed, headed by Mr. Peter Donaldson, and Mr. William Fife jnr. was given the task of designing a Scottish yacht for the honour of the thistle. She was christened CALLUNA and was built at very short notice by the firm of A. & J. Inglis. Mr. Peter Donaldson acted as representative owner and was supported by his brother Mr. Robert M. Donaldson.

But in truth Calluna does not appear to have had much luck in that season of 1893. In her first race on the River Thames she went ashore on the Ovens shoal; in her second she was dismasted before the start. True she won the Channel race from Dover to Boulogne that year but only after Vendetta, Valkyrie and Britannia had been in collision. In the Royal Mersey Regatta she was a non-starter owing to her anchor fouling. In the Royal Irish Y.C.'s Queen's Cup she was disabled by a main-boom broken in gybing. In the Cowes Town Cup she was in collision with a steam yacht, suffered damage to her jackyard and split her mainsail from gaff to boom. In this picture, taken at Cowes in August 1893, she is enjoying better luck as she reaches out ahead of Iverna, who has Valkyrie II almost abeam to weather, in front of a north-west breeze up towards the Calshot Light Vessel. Valkyrie appears to have 26 people on deck and her spinnaker boom is rigged. Calluna has one man at least up the main shroud ratlines, just below the spreaders. The fiddle bow of Iverna betrays the older boat and shows her not so distant descent from the straight stemmed cutters of the 1850's. She doesn't appear to be making any preparations to set a 'kite'.

By 1895, Iverna was outclassed by Britannia, Valkyrie II and Satanita. Her greatest season was her first in 1890, when her rival was Thistle—owned by Mr. Bell who had been a member of the syndicate which had built her for the America's Cup challenge against Volunteer in 1887. Now refitted and her sparring somewhat reduced Thistle reappeared under Mr. Bell's flag. In that first year it all went Thistle's way to begin with, but constant tuning and alteration —Iverna did away with the centreboard she was originally equipped with—brought the two boats much closer together. Iverna worked up to 20 victories against Thistle's 22. In 1891 there was a falling off in the big class which floated only Iverna, Valkyrie and Maid Marion, the former Yarana. Iverna won 22 prizes in this year against Valkyrie's 15. In 1892 the class was reduced to Iverna and the now renamed Thistle, the Kaiser's yacht Meteor. Iverna again showed her innate superiority over her old rival by winning 15 matches over 11. 1893 saw the birth of the new big cutters and the ascendendancy of the designs of G. L. Watson—engendered by Dunraven's new challenge for the America's Cup. Iverna's day was done and with her a chapter in yachting's history of which the highlight was necessarily the schooner America.

The third yacht in picture is Dunraven's Valkyrie II, built as we have stated as an America's Cup challenger. She was to say the least an unlucky yacht. Her first races showed that she and her 'chummy' ship Britannia were very evenly matched. The relationship—same designer, same builders, same year—was to go even closer than was comfortable. Early in the 1893 season in the Dover-Boulogne Cross-Channel Race she was involved in the famous triple collision. It happened that Vendetta, a smaller Summers & Payne 76-tonner, crossed the start line first in a smart north-easterly breeze but collided with Valkyrie, losing her topmast in the process. Britannia then collided with Valkyrie, her bowsprit fouling the latter's rigging and at the same time breaking Vendetta's bowsprit. The three cutters were now hopelessly entangled —and they were large yachts by any standards. Britannia's mainsail, pressing against Vendetta's port crosstree, split from boom to gaff. It was Valkyrie's crew who finally succeeded in cutting away Britannia's bowsprit to free this log-jam of fine ships. In a later Royal Clyde match, Britannia was involved in a port and starboard incident and subsequent collision with Valkyrie and Britannia was disqualified. In the succeeding year 1894 Valkyrie was rammed and sunk by Satanita in the Clyde. This famous incident is dealt with elsewhere in this book, so there is no point in repeating it here. But it was a sad and melancholy thing to end such a fine ship's life so early in her career. (P. 54-55.)

Calluna: Owner - Clyde syndicate represented by Mr. Peter Donaldson: Designer - W. Fife jnr. Builder - A. & J. Inglis, Glasgow, 1893. Length B.P. 106.6 ft. Length W.L. 81.95 ft. Breadth 24.3 ft. Depth 11.2 ft. Tons T.M. 258.

Iverna: Owner - Mr. John Jameson (Dublin): Designer - A. Richardson: Builder - J. G. Fay & Co. Ltd., Southampton, 1890. Length B.P. 98 ft. Length W.L. 84.7 ft. Breadth 19 ft. Depth 10.7 ft. Tons T.M. 152.

Valkyrie II. Owner - The Earl of Dunraven: Designer - G.L. Watson: Builder - D. & W. Henderson, Glasgow, 1893. Length B.P 106.55 ft. Length W.L. 86.8 ft. Breadth 21.7 ft. Depth 12.95 ft.

$\mathcal{N}$AVAHOE was designed by N. G. Herreshoff and built at his yard at Bristol, Rhode Island, for an American owner Royal Phelps Carroll in 1893—and that year was a memorable one in yachting history. The Prince of Wales (later King Edward VII) came out with Britannia and the Earl of Dunraven's Valkyrie II challenged for the America's Cup. Carroll announced his intention of crossing the Atlantic in the opposite direction to challenge for the Royal Victoria Gold Cup and the Cape May and Brenton Reef Cups. Navahoe, rating 156·70 and setting 10,815 sq.ft., arrived in British waters before Cowes Week. She showed remarkable qualities on a broad reach and a run, but Britannia, who had been chosen to defend these trophies, was reckoned to have the legs of her to windward. The latter won the Gold Cup with little difficulty and the Brenton Reef race was set for September 12 over a course from a point off the Needles, across Channel, round Cherbourg breakwater and back. There was a fine breeze and some sea but two hours after the start 25 miles had been logged. In spite of getting the start by 54 seconds, Britannia was just astern of the challenger through the breakwater but overhauled her on the return. Nevertheless Navahoe was seldom more than 150 yards astern. This race was bedevilled by one of those committee incidents which were capable of marring such events. The steamer on the finishing line could not be anchored off the Needles and was therefore brought into Alum Bay inside the Needles. Britannia with her start advantage deducted was declared the winner by $2\frac{1}{2}$ seconds. Carroll protested that the steamer was off-station and that the time difference between the two yachts was less. A committee of the Royal Yacht Squadron heard the protest and awarded the race to Navahoe. Three days later the Cape May Cup was held over the same course except that the start and finish were in Alum Bay. This was not so exciting an event being run in calms and fog before a north-east breeze in which Britannia got the best of the start, went on to lead and to win. Navahoe was nevertheless a very successful yacht. In the great year of 1893 she won six of her eighteen starts. She was bought around about 1901 by George W. Watjen, a shipowner and banker of Bremen and New York. Between then and 1906 she won 75 prizes—all of them first flags except five.

Navahoe: Length O.A. 126.0 ft. Length W.L. 86.94 ft. Breadth 24.0 ft. Draft 12.6 ft. Tons T.M. 114.2.

*T*HERE can be little left to say about the greatest racing yacht of them all and certainly not by a 'late comer' such as this author. But I do remember her—and remember her racing although I was a small boy at the time. She was yet another yacht of 1893, designed by George Lennox Watson (to give that great man his full name) and Clyde-built by Henderson's for the Prince of Wales. She was composite built and in fact her scantlings were lighter than those required 35 years later by Lloyd's for first-class racing yachts! She was of course still racing and still winning then. Her original sail plan comprised approximately 10,000 sq.ft. and her height of mast was some 110 feet. The story goes that the main spar was stepped root end aloft!

We have already referred to 1893 as being a vintage yachting year. BRITANNIA's chief competitors were Satanita, Valkyrie II (a sort of half-sister and only a trifle smaller), Calluna and Iverna. Of these 'the Cup' challenger Valkyrie was her closest rival. However, there can be little doubt that Britannia was the better boat of the two. In the paragraphs on Vigilant we speculate a little as to what might have happened had Britannia been the challenger. She sealed herself firmly in the hearts of all British yachtsmen by getting the better of the American yacht Navahoe who campaigned in British South Coast waters while Vigilant was preparing to defend the Cup across the Atlantic. Britannia's record of 33 firsts out of 43 starts in her first season was a remarkable one, and she won over £2,200 in prize money which was a considerable sum and probably worth seven times that nowadays.

In the succeeding year she had a tremendous tussle in British regattas with the successful American defender Vigilant who had come across to try her luck. By and large she succeeded where Valkyrie II had failed. A lot of this story is told in the notes on Vigilant and on Satanita. In 1895 she had many close races with the beautiful Fife yacht Ailsa which she first met out in the Mediterranean. Incidentally, on her passage out she logged on an occasion 26 sea miles in two hours. This is not a yacht record—the schooner Atlantic racing from New York to England averaged 14.2 knots for 24 hours—but it is a very high speed for the time on a waterline of 88 feet. Britannia won 32 prizes in 39 starts but her races with Ailsa were mostly very closely fought. She also notched over £3,000 in cash, apart from her lockerful of cups and trophies. I quote the late John Scott Hughes as saying that she cost about £10,000 to build—so her prize money in her first few seasons certainly paid for her upkeep and went quite a way towards the cost of her construction. What would Britannia cost to build today?

In 1901 Queen Victoria died and the Prince of Wales ascended the throne. Britannia was sold to Sir Richard Williams-Bulkeley, who cut her down and used her mostly for cruising. The King soon regretted parting with her and bought her back. However, the first years of the new century were not very active ones for first class racing and, perhaps because those in charge thought she was too old, she missed the revival which came with Nyria, White Heather II and Shamrock III in 1906. She raced again occasionally in 1913 and 1914 but only against inferior opposition. Her racing career was resumed after the Great War.

The Britannia thread runs through many of the stories in this book and it would be mere repetition to put them all down again. She was the epitome of the big cutters from 1893 up to the outbreak of war and for 20 years the history of these tremendous yachts has the name Britannia written largely across it.

The photograph itself is interesting and full of drama. It has been published before but I don't know whether the anecdote connected with it has been told. Britannia is just preparing to gybe round the mark. The spinnaker boom is being run out. There is more in it than that. There is a man overboard to leeward. At the foot of the mast one of the crew is throwing a rope. It caught round the swimmer's ankle and he was hauled back on board over the transom. (P. 60-61.)

Britannia: Length O.A. 123 ft. Length W.L. 88 ft. Beam 23.3 ft. Draft 15 ft. Tons T.M. 221.

$\mathcal{T}$HE two yachts are WHITE ROSE, nearer the camera, and RED ROVER. They are the small racing yachts—the One Raters—of the Sail Area Rule. The rule held sway between 1887 and 1895 and the photograph was taken in the last year of its run. As can be seen they were small, wet boats—and great fun. As befits her name, White Rose was owned by the Duke of York. He ordered the boat to be built in five days—and this was done. I think one would be quite safe in describing this as something of a record! The single batten stretching right across the head of the mainsail from the yard to the leach is interesting.

Volante 1852

(Colour Lithograph.
E. C. Dolby after C. S. Robins)

This 59-tonner — a small yacht for her times — was built in 1850. She won the 200-guinea cup presented by the Royal Thames Yacht Club in 1852. The preceding year Volante was among the America's opponents, but a collision with Freak forced her to abandon the race. Ten years later a new owner had her lengthened and gave her a new entry at the stem in accordance with the fashion of the day. She scored many victories right through to 1869, when on September 12 that year she dragged her anchor and was wrecked on Ryde Sands.

Sveridge and Rosalind - 1853

(Oil Painting. Macpherson Collection)

The schooner Sveridge of 280 tons was built in 1852 on the plans of the America for Thomas Bartlett, Commodore of the Royal London Yacht Club. This canvas depicts the spectacular finish of the Royal Thames Yacht Club's race in 1853 in which no less than six schooners completed the course from Gravesend out to the Mouse and back in under five hours. Sveridge carried away her fore-topmast but in spite of this crossed the line 25 seconds ahead of Rosalind.

*T*HE 20-rater DEIDRE was one of the Earl of Dunraven's veritable fleet of yachts. She was G. L. Watson designed and built by Reid & Co. of Glasgow in 1893 at the same time as the Earl was building Valkyrie II. With 21 prizes in 35 starts she was second only to Dragon III, also a new boat but Fife designed. In 1894 she came into the hands of that celebrated sporting peer, the Earl of Lonsdale, who had been 'blooded' for sailing by Dunraven himself. As the photograph shows, the 20 Raters were fine, competent boats —and this is what they enjoyed best of all, reaching in a fresh breeze. She will be doing about 11 knots and, although only the big plate photo will probably show this, there is a lady in the cockpit with her hat firmly belayed to her head with a scarf. (P.66-67.)

*F*REDA was a real old-fashioned one. She was designed by Dixon Kemp and built at Payne's yard at Southampton in 1885. She was a fine, hefty big yawl of 120 tons Thames Measurement. She could travel nevertheless. In 1899 she is spoken of as the winner of the German Emperor's Cup. Vessels of this size with the power to stand up to their sailplan were great boats on reaching courses. Here they are making the best of a reach eastwards from Cowes towards Ryde and Spithead in quite fresh conditions but with hardly more than a degree or two of heel.

*V*IGILANT was the successful Cup defender of 1893 under a syndicate headed by C. O. Iselin against Valkyrie II. She was Herreshoff designed and built and set the colossal sail area of 11,600 sq.ft. in her rig. Her rating was 168·5.

The 1894 season started fairly tamely after the excitements of 1893 with BRITANNIA and Iverna the first afloat. These two were then joined by Satanita. But with the appearance of Vigilant the interest became intense. The successful Cup defender of the year before arrived in British waters under the flag of George and Howard Gould. The whole yachting world was agog to see what would be the outcome between her and the defeated Valkyrie in the waters over here —and perhaps even more interested in the meetings which would inevitably take place between her and Britannia. Valkyrie joined the big class on the Clyde in early July but on this occasion Vigilant did not enter an appearance. But she did turn out in the following Clyde regatta. Unfortunately this 'meeting of giants' was marred by the collision between Satanita and Valkyrie in which the latter was cut down to the waterline and sunk and a crewman killed. The race was however completed, Vigilant persistently lee-bowing Britannia and leading by 2 minutes on the first round. Britannia however got a lift on the last round and won by 36 seconds. This was not a particularly meritorious victory but it was the first of a brilliant series of races between the two yachts. Vigilant's enormous sail spread gave her superiority downwind but it appeared that Britannia could hold her on other points and even seemed the better boat of the two in light, variable breezes. As if to settle which of these splendid vessels was the 'queen of the seas', Lord Wolverton presented a trophy in August for a match race between the two. This however proved abortive when Vigilant's centreboard jammed. It was found later that the slot in her keel had closed in to 2 ½ inches from 4 inches, doubtless from hitting bottom.

In September Vigilant challenged for the Cape May Cup. It will be remembered that in the year before, 1893, another Herreshoff yacht Navahoe had challenged for this trophy as well as the Brenton Reef Cup. Britannia had won the latter by a few seconds only to have the race awarded against her on protest concerning the placing of the finishing line. She had however repulsed the American challenge for the Cape May in a race run in calms and flukey winds. The 1894 event therefore created great interest. However as it turned out this too proved abortive. Two days before the race, Vigilant was beating up West Channel when she touched in Alum Bay. Her centreboard subsequently fell out in deep water. The challenge was withdrawn although Mr. Gould expressed willingness to sail the race without the plate and shipping 4 tons of ballast—the equivalent weight!—in lieu.

In spite of Britannia's fine record, Vigilant was sailing under disadvantages and did not have the best of the luck. In all the two yachts were very evenly matched with perhaps Britannia slightly the better of the two. It is interesting to speculate what might have happened if it had been the Prince of Wales who had challenged for the 1893 attempt—and if he had succeeded! This photograph might show the result of the final race of such a hypothetical challenge—both tremendous yachts driving for the line at maximum speed with every stitch of canvas set. (P. 70-71.)

*T*HERE is not much to say about this picture except to remark that it is a most unusual one. It is of course foreshortened but it does show the tremendous beam of these yachts—over 26 feet in this case—which together with a large volume of deep lead gave the necessary power to carry their colossal sailplans. VALKYRIE set 13,000 sq.ft. Note too that the chainplates for the main rigging are not at maximum beam, which is located some feet further aft. The bow overhang must have been enormous. The boots of the workmen on the staging over the stem are reflected in the water a long distance ahead of the stem's bobstay-fitting on Valkyrie's waterline.

Vigilant: Length O.A. 128 ft. Length W.L. 86.12 ft. Breadth 26.4 ft. Draft 14 ft. Tons T.M. 144.

*T*HE American yacht VIGILANT, successful defender of the America's Cup in 1893 against Valkyrie II, was always a smart ship. When she came over in the succeeding year she was Britannia's great rival.

This 'portrait' of her in dry-dock shows what a graceful shape Nathaniel Herreshoff gave her. And they had discipline aboard these yachts. See how neatly all her running rigging is set up and rope tails coiled and stowed. Note also the appearance of the sheet winch on deck!

It is said that Vigilant had a crew of 70 in the second Cup race of 1894, as against 35 aboard Valkyrie, when she came through from two minutes astern at the weathermark by setting a spinnaker and a jackyarder and shaking out her reefs in half a gale. (P. 74-75.)

*V*IGILANT leads BRITANNIA on this occasion in 1894 but all season the racing was close and hotly contested with Britannia, who had just that little bit more luck, proving the more successful of the two. Vigilant was incidentally a centre-boarder, a feature which as it so happened gave her trouble when challenging Britannia for the Cape May Cup. But under the flag of George and Howard Gould who brought her across from the States she was well and truly raced. Observe practically all the crew prone on the deck and the helmsman crouched behind the great wheel.

Britannia close behind seems to be holding a slightly higher course and it is doubtful, if it were necessary, whether Vigilant has room to tack across her bows. (P. 76-77.)

*L*IKE the photograph of Ulerin this shot is slightly deceiving. The loftiness of the sparring and the spread of canvas makes THELMA appear much larger than she was. The figure on the counter, the one standing in the lee scuppers and the third crouched at the weather rail by the shrouds belie the scale effect of the rig. Thelma was a Fife designed 20 Rater of 1894. There was a strong class of these in that year of which the most successful was Mr. F. B. Jameson's Luna, which started 53 times and collected 20 first prizes, 9 seconds and 3 thirds.

$\mathcal{V}$ALKYRIE III was the Dunraven challenger for the America's Cup which was concerned in the famous or infamous incidents involving that unlucky earl—unlucky at all events as far as that elusive trophy was concerned.

The sole topic of the late winter of 1895 was the new challenge and the hopes of this new Watson designed yacht building at D. & W. Henderson of Glasgow. She joined the big class at the Clyde regattas. In the Mudhook Yacht Club's events on July 3 over a principally reaching course in a fine breeze she was beaten by both Britannia and Ailsa. Valkyrie III was a fast light weather yacht particularly to windward. She was however excessively tender and showed up badly when reaching in a breeze.

She left directly from the Clyde for the Cup with absurdly little opportunity for tuning up. In all respects this was a disastrous challenge. The appropriately named American yacht Defender had all the luck that was going in the first race as well as the inestimable advantage of spectator fleet and excursion steamers severely cutting up Valkyrie III's wind on the run back to the line. The second race was over the triangular course in light weather through smooth water—conditions much to Valkyrie III's liking. She was first in by 1 minute 16 seconds (46 seconds on corrected time), but was disqualified on protest. When reaching in at the start to pass close to the markboat she was obliged to luff to avoid Defender. As she swung to her helm her boom fouled and carried away the American's starboard topmast shroud. This was instantly put to rights aboard Defender but the protest was won—and the race lost for the Earl of Dunraven. Worse was to follow in the third race when Dunraven started and immediately hauled down his flag and went home. Allegations followed of illegal changes in ballasting of the American yacht after measurement which were refuted by the New York Yacht Club. Nothing but ill-feeling came out of this attempt to win the Cup and it took a long time for the bitterness it generated to dissolve.

Still in these later days we must be grateful that Valkyrie III was built to give us this superb photograph of her sailing on trials in Scottish waters and in real 'Scottish weather'! Shortly after it was taken Valkyrie III lost her mast, so there was some wind that day. (P. 80-81.)

We have already noted the story of the disastrous cup series between Valkyrie III and Defender, but this is the historic photograph of the Earl of Dunraven's challenger coming home to finish first by 46 seconds on corrected time in the second race of the series, only to have the protest lodged against her for the foul in manœuvring at the start. The conditions at the time were most difficult and made even more awkward for these large vessels by spectator vessels which included a large steamer wandering all over the course.

Truth to tell the Race Committee made a big effort to compromise this protest—Dunraven's earlier allegations of illegal changes in ballast aboard Defender after measurement had nettled the Americans and had been clearly refuted. In spite of this rancour the New York Yacht Club went out of their way to suggest that the race be resailed but Dunraven would have none of this gesture and the committee were left with little alternative but to uphold Defender and award her the race. Dunraven complained vehemently about the behaviour of the spectator fleet and threatened retirement from the third race—a threat he duly executed. Still here is one of those few moments of glory in many, many years when a challenger crossed the finishing line ahead of the defender. It is possible that Valkyrie III was in any case as good a boat as her American rival. To a modern mind the photograph demonstrates most vividly the weakness in the gaff cutter rig—especially aft of the mast. The 'twist' in the mainsail is something which could never be accepted nowadays. To put it simply—it's either a right trim at the top or a right trim at the bottom, but they can't both be right! (P. 82-83)

Valkyrie III: Length B.P. 100.7 ft. Length W.L. 88.65 ft. Breadth 25.7 ft. Depth 11.5 ft. Sail Area 13.027 sq. ft. Tons T.M. 263.

$\mathcal{N}$oт many people will have seen this photograph before —Shamrock, the first one, in trouble. This occurred in the second race for the 1899 America's Cup challenge. The 'upper-yardmen' standing on the spreaders have got a good view of the problem. It is the topmast which has carried away. What might be described as a clean break! The jackyard took part of the punishment and now there's only the business of getting it down on deck. The mainsail luff is attached to the mast by mast hoops of steamed ash or elm made to fit the spar as closely as possible. It's odd to think now of the days before mast track and mast groove—perhaps in a few years we shall think that wooden masts are rather old fashioned things like mast hoops! Shamrock had lost the first race of the series, was disabled in this race and went on to lose the third. She was never in proper trim—though this might in some large measure be due to Fife, her designer, falling ill and being unable to supervise her tuning.

THIS was the scene shortly after the incident at the start of the second race of the 1895 America's Cup series between DEFENDER and the Earl of Dunraven's Valkyrie III. The Americans had already won the first race when the spectator fleet, following closely on the heels of the trailing challenger as the yachts ran back to the line, severely hampered Valkyrie. It was said that spectator boats and particularly a large steamer in the vicinity of the line were the prime cause of this mishap. Anyhow Valkyrie found herself reaching at speed down the line to pass close to the committee boat. She luffed to keep clear and as her stern swung the end of her boom, which projected some feet over the arch-board of her counter, caught Defender's topmast backstay. The result you see. The damage was soon put right and although Defender finished only 1 minute 16 seconds behind she even recovered some of this on handicap correction to lose by 46 seconds.

Valkyrie III was disqualified on protest—though in fact the Committee suggested a resail. However what with Dunraven's allegations of illegal ballast changes, everybody's tempers were fully aroused. The Earl refused to resail and withdrew shortly after the start of the third race. This challenge was a disaster and left a rotten taste in everybody's mouth. It was left to Sir Thomas Lipton and the Shamrock dynasty to put relations between the yachtsmen of the two countries back on a good footing. (P. 86-87.)

IN contrast to some of our photographs where comparatively small yachts look vast—I was thinking of that great picture of Ulerin—here is one which makes a large one look smaller than she is. CARESS is over 70 feet long and some 78 tons Thames Measurement. She was one of the new '40 Raters' of 1895 and designed by G. L. Watson. Another new '40' of that year was the new Fife first class yacht Ailsa. Britannia, Namara and Corsair made up the fleet. But of the three '40's' proper—Carina was the third—Isolde was the fastest. Caress was a good boat but somewhat too large in hull measurement for her rating. She needed in truth to be slightly smaller and to be rigged with a little more sail to do really well among the 40's. In 1896 with changes stimulated by the change to the new Y.R.A. Linear Rating Rule she had her sail area increased, came into the first class and did better on her time allowance. One understands that such problems in for instance today's R.O.R.C. classifications can be exactly the same!

*I*N 1890 racing was hot stuff and the starts were hotly fought affairs. These '20 Raters'—on the right, PENITENT, then AUDREY, SAMPHIRE, ISOLDE and an unidentified boat on the extreme left of the photograph—show this to be indeed true. Audrey was one of the Earl of Dunraven's veritable fleet of yachts. The peer owned another 20 Rater, Deidre, subsequently bought by the Earl of Lonsdale. Samphire, a new yacht in 1896, was interesting for reason of her light construction and bulb keel. She was a Sibbick boat and built along the same ideas of another 20 Rater, Niagara, designed a year earlier by Nat Herreshoff. Isolde was really a sister ship of Niagara and was owned by Baron von Zedwitz. She came on the scene at the same time as the Kaiser's 20 Rater Vineta, and was involved in a tragic accident in 1896, when her owner was killed. This occasion is referred to in the notes on Meteor II, but there are additional details which might be mentioned here. The 20 Raters, or '52 Footers' as they had been termed under an earlier rule, were finishing the first round of their course at Cowes. Isolde led, closely followed by The Saint. Britannia and Meteor were coming up astern at the head of the big class, Britannia seeking to pass to windward and Meteor to leeward. Isolde luffed in an attempt to get to weather of Britannia in order to avoid being blanketed. At this moment The Saint fouled Isolde's backstay and the latter was thrown across Meteor's bow. In the ensuing collision Meteor's main-boom swept Isolde's deck and von Zedwitz was mortally hurt. But the scene we witness here is remote from that tragedy and everything is set and ready for a close and exciting race. (P. 90-91.)

*B*ONA was a very elegant cutter from the drawing board of G. L. Watson, who made her first appearance in the Clyde regattas of 1897. She was built for the Duke of Abruzzi in the yard of D. & W. Henderson at Glasgow and for a long time had Peter Henderson as her helmsman. She met the Kaiser's Meteor in the big handicap class for the first time when the venue of the races shifted to North Ireland. The race between the two boats was close enough from the point of view of the corrected result after handicap, though there was a fair amount of water between the two. Bona's Linear Rating was 80: that of Meteor nearer 100. But there's no doubt that Bona was a remarkably quick boat, particularly in light breezes—although she seems to have been favoured by the Y.R.A. time scale. In strong winds she was out-distanced by other competitors.

In 1898 she started her season on the Riviera where, in prevailing light conditions, she bested Satanita. On her return to England her most redoubtable adversary turned out to be Ailsa. In the following year her chief rival was Rainbow, but Bona gave her few chances of winning. Later in the season Meteor came to the Solent newly rigged as a yawl, and with a reduction in time allowance from that level which she had previously had to accord Bona. It was this more than any other factor which swung the balance in Meteor's favour.

Bona gained one of her most sparkling victories when she beat seventeen other starters in the German Emperor's Cup at Cowes in 1903. The following years saw a diminution of handicap racing. Owners were tiring of races between yachts of very different size and characteristic. They were already voicing their opinions on this score to the Y.R.A. and these were in turn to lead to the Y.R.A. convening the International Conference of 1906 and the subsequent adoption of the International Metre Rule.

Bona: Length B.P. 89.0 ft. Length W.L. 75.8 ft. Breadth 18.0 ft. Depth 11.7 ft. Tons T.M. 122.

ETEOR II was perhaps G. L. Watson's masterpiece—and this is a magnificent photograph of a magnificent boat. She was designed to the Y.R.A. rule which replaced the length/sail area rule. Her owner was the Kaiser William II. His motive in building her was simply to tan the hide off Britannia. This shot, with the Hohenzollern Eagle proudly flown aloft, was taken in 1896, the year of her first appearance on the racing scene. She joined the cutter fleet on the Thames in June and it was at once very clear that the German Emperor had got himself a very fast boat indeed. She won all her races before sailing over to Kiel during that month. A little later she appeared on the Clyde, escorted by a torpedo-boat of the Imperial German Navy—one of the reasons for William II's involvement in big class yacht racing was his demonstrative challenge to British sea-power.

Meteor's record got better and better as the regattas moved south. But her progress was marred and cut short by a fatal accident in a race under the burgee of the Royal Albert Yacht Club in which the Baron von Zedwitz lost his life. Von Zedwitz was aboard Isolde when she was involved in a luffing match, and a minor collision with The Saint carried her right across Meteor's bows. Meteor's main-boom scythed Isolde's deck from stem to stern. The crew saved their lives by leaping overboard, but von Zedwitz was trapped by the boom as it fell. He died aboard the steam-yacht Bohemia while being taken to Ryde. Neither the Kaiser's Meteor nor the Prince of Wales' Britannia raced again that season.

In the succeeding year racing for the big cutters lacked interest. Meteor in her contests with Bona found herself unable to compete with the new Y.R.A. time scale. In 1898 she raced on the Riviera but again found herself beaten by Bona who was a great light weather boat. However in 1899 she came out as a yawl. She was as fast as she ever was and, with her reduced time allowance, showed herself to be Bona's mistress. This was the year of Tommy Lipton's first challenge for the America's Cup with his first Shamrock. It is easy to see that British preoccupation with the two Shamrock challenges and then the death of Queen Victoria in 1901 drew public attention away from His Imperial Majesty—hard cheddar. In 1902 he abandoned Meteor II, who passed to the German Navy, and placed an order in the United States—for political reasons more than anything else—for the schooner Meteor III. She was launched, as scheduled, by the daughter of the President of the United States. Barely ten years were now to pass before the British Empire and Germany, whose ruling houses were so closely related, came to war and the face of the world was changed. (P. 94-95.)

AINBOW was designed by G. L. Watson and built at Glasgow in 1898 by D. & W. Henderson for C. L. Orr Ewing, Member of Parliament. This is an exceptional photograph, full of grace and power, of Rainbow racing close-hauled at Cowes in a fine full-sail breeze in August of her first season.

Rainbow was *not* designed as a racing yacht. She was simply a yacht. Her Linear Rating of 114.53 didn't make it easy for her to win prizes after the time correction had been applied. But she had a very large sail-area of 13,500 sq.ft. and on her good days gave ample demonstration of the speed of which she was capable. In the Royal Yacht Squadron's Queen's Cup—with little close-winded racing as it so happened—she covered 50 miles in 3 hours 52 minutes and 46 seconds. Later her rating under the new International Rule was established at 30.59 Metres. In 1904 she passed into the hands of the Verein Seefahrt Hamburg under the name Hamburg.

Rainbow: Length B.P. 132.7 ft. Length W.L. 116.2 ft. Breath 23.9 ft. Depth 14.1 ft. Tons T.M. 331.

*T*HIS should have been the Photograph of the Year!—of 1899. There was an awful mess for everyone to clear up each time something didn't go according to the book up aloft aboard the great cutters. This is Lipton's Shamrock—the first one—in trouble and with her mainsail spread all over the deck. Her jackyard topsail is also involved in this Irish wake.

It's not easy to see what was the root cause of this spectacular mishap—and were telephoto lenses invented in those days? It looks as though the gaff has broken off about six or eight feet from the gaff jaws and that this has brought down with it the jackyard topsail—the upper spar of which has broken and the lower become entangled in the mainsail. For those on deck this must have been like a cathedral spire tumbling down on top of them. The crew are immensely active. There's one shinning up the rigging like a Pacific Islander in search of coconuts. A second swings down the steel wire-rope gaff halyards. A third stands on the shoulders of his comrade at the broken end of the gaff to try and free the sail. Four are struggling with the remains of the spar at the mast and another is tight-rope walking on the remains of the spar itself to clear some of the wire entanglement. There are approximately 16 others beavering around, each with his own particular part of the problem to solve. Was the phrase 'and the best of British luck' invented at this time or did the Shamrock of Ireland have a pixie hand in the affair?

Shamrock made 260 tons T.M. She was built by John I. Thornycroft to Fife's design. Many pundits considered her a better challenger for the America's Cup than the 1901, Watson designed Shamrock II. In fact when she met her successor on windward work there was no doubt as to which was the faster boat—and even less when it blew fresh and there was a bit of a sea.

COLUMBIA defended the America's Cup twice—in 1899 against Shamrock and in 1901 against Shamrock II. Columbia was designed by Herreshoff for the syndicate headed by Pierpoint Morgan and Oliver Iselin. The syndicate's skipper was the redoubtable Charlie Barr, a Scot before he became a naturalised American. The photograph was taken during the 1899 challenge which was easily won by Columbia. Here her crew are in the process of hoisting the spinnaker. Clearly visible are 27 crew—and there are probably more around and about that mast on the weather side. The spinnaker boom is hardly a toothpick and the mainsheet block at deck is a great deal bigger than a man's head. The spinnaker is on its way aloft. Once hoisted the tack will be *hauled* out to the end of that boom. Seven men are tailed onto the boom guy—they're there and all set to take the shock. Racing was not particularly a performance of protocol in those days—nevertheless the crews were dressed in white and some of the officers are there at their stations in stiff collars and bow ties. (P. 100-101.)

HERE is a gayer picture of the first Shamrock than the last we saw. It was taken in United States waters at the beginning of the struggle against Columbia. Such yachts carried enormous crews in order to deal with their enormous sail areas. Looking at the photo I suppose one should be surprised that Shamrock has two mainmasts. Not so! The foremost of those two great spars is the jackyard, ready for hoisting. In the original Beken plate it is possible to identify a crewman sitting at the spreaders. He was there to control the sending aloft of that jackyard and its vast topsail. Right outboard at the end of the bowsprit the flying jib is made ready—the foredeck crew are coming back inboard. Note that Shamrock was tiller steered. The helmsman is *marching* up the deck to put the helm to weather and persuade Shamrock to pay off. As to the main-boom it is probably bending under it's own weight, and there are five lazy-jacks deployed along its length to support the spar when hoisting or lowering the sail. (P. 102-103.)

WE have already seen a photograph of the first schooner Cetonia, owned by Sir E. Guinness (later Lord Iveagh), racing against Amphitrite. Cetonia was built at 203 tons T.M. by Ratsey in 1873. She figures in Lloyd's Yacht Register right up to 1906—the year in which another splendid yacht of the same name in Lord Iveagh's ownership appeared in the Register. It is the second one that we are looking at now.
She was built from the design of J.M. Soper by Camper & Nicholson in 1902 for Mr. S. M. Singer of New York. Her original sailplan of 6,560 sq. ft. was increased first to 9,860 sq. ft. and then to 11,000 sq.ft. and a Linear Rating of 95.30. Lord Iveagh bought her from Mr. Singer in 1906 and CETONIA was still in his ownership in 1915.
The longevity of more than one of these marvellous vessels of the great days of yachting and the fidelity of the owners to their vessels is a remarkable feature of the scene. John Scott Hughes wrote: '...of all the things fashioned by the hand of man, perhaps it was a boat which came nearest his heart.' One recalls Arrow, Fiona, Bloodhound—and of course Britannia. The Cetonias must have been of this squadron. Lord Iveagh kept the first of the name and the second remained with him sixteen years before she was sold to Gilbert A. Tonge. But speaking of longevity, I have a snapshot of Cetonia taken in 1930 when she was owned by Lord Stalbridge and rigged as a three-masted staysail schooner! And she was still listed in Lloyd's Register of Yachts in 1939.
Cetonia was never a brilliant racing yacht but she was certain by a superb cruiser in the grand manner. And here's a curious historical footnote—a commentary on our times. In 1934 she appeared in a broker's announcement. This splendid vessel of 295 tons Thomas Measurement was offered for sail at a price of £4,000—a rate of under £14 a ton!

Cetonia: Length 120.3 ft. Length W.L. 100.0 ft. Breadth 24.0 ft. Depth 11.7 ft. Tons T.M. 295.

$\mathcal{T}$HIS dramatic picture shows what a mess there is to clear up when a mast and over 14,000 sq.ft. of sail come tumbling down. It was taken in 1901 in the Solent and the new King, Edward VII, was aboard at the time. SHAMROCK II was of course the second America's Cup challenge to carry Sir Thomas Lipton's colours. The original Shamrock which had lost to Columbia in 1899 had been Fife designed and built at J. I. Thornycroft's Chiswick yard on the Thames. For his new yacht Lipton went to G. L. Watson and built at W. Denny & Bros., Dumbarton. Shamrock II carried much the same measurements as the earlier yacht. Her length between perpendiculars was only 2 feet 6 inches greater and there were only inches in waterline and breadth measurements.

Her first trials, racing against the older Shamrock, were not encouraging. The new yacht proved slower in anything of a breeze and especially in lumpy water. Strangely enough this situation was paralleled in the United States where the new prospective defender Constitution also lost her mast and showed less reliability than the old Columbia. Shamrock II did improve but the Americans decided it was safer to select the previous defender once again.

In the first race for the Cup in light winds it was Sir Thomas's challenger who led at the weather mark. But in the dying breeze she was passed and was led home by 37 seconds (1 minute 20 seconds on corrected time). In the stronger 12-knot north-easterly wind of the second race she was again beaten and it seemed that Columbia was certainly the faster reaching yacht and possibly also to windward in that weight of wind. The third race provided a moderate breeze, steady at first but becoming flukey later. Shamrock II ran down to the lee mark faster and turned 49 seconds in the lead. If she could have held this she would have saved her time, but alas, she lost this ground on the beat, scrambling over the line first by 2 seconds and losing by 41 seconds on corrected time. So the eleventh challenge was thrown back in the short space of one week. It was generally thought that Shamrock II could have won had she been more carefully tuned at home and had she been as equally well handled as the defender. (P. 106-107.)

Shamrock II: Length B.P. 108.0 ft. Length W.L. 89.25 ft. Breadth 24.4 ft. Depth 10.0 ft. Tons T.M. 265.

WE have a shot of Bona on her own. We have one of Creole racing Britomart. Now here is a fine storming one of BONA and CREOLE, as both yachts smoke along at maximum speed with their lee rails down.

Bona was in her first year, 1897. She was remarkably fast, very handsome and was lucky with her Y.R.A. time-scale handicap. She was a Watson designed '83-Rater' and was launched in 1897. Creole was also Watson but was launched seven years earlier as one of the '40's' under the old Sail Area Rule. Perhaps the difference in age is best expressed by the different bows —Creole to weather and the newer Bona to leeward. Both were most distinguished yachts. Creole won the German Emperor's Cup fourteen years after she was built. Bona was a famous light weather specialist and collected scalps from Meteor, Satanita and Rainbow in her day. She was tiller steered and is here being controlled by yoke-lines and tackles rigged from the end of her tiller, with her helmsman standing in the lee scuppers and the rest of the crew on the weather deck.

*T*HIS is an interesting photograph of some interesting yachts —EILUN, L'AMOUREUSE, HARMONY, ALMIDA and JEAN. They were vessels of 24 tons Thames Measurement—about 40 feet on the waterline and carrying approximately 2,000 sq.ft. of sail. Five can be seen in the picture. Only six were ever built. Of the five musketeers ALMIDA, the oldest, was designed and built by Fife at Fairlie in Scotland in 1893. The others were A. Mylne designed, three being built at Stone Brothers of Brightlingsea and one at Forrest & Son at Wivenhoe in 1903, both English East Coast yards. Yet these yachts became known

as the South Coast One Designs—no relation to the present day S.C.O.D.'s who merely borrowed the title. Here they are then in the Solent—obviously impeccably maintained and very keenly raced. The crew on No. 1 is really sweating on that mainsheet as they claim room at the mark in that summer of 1904.

Why, in modern parlance, didn't they 'catch on'? The Earl of Albemarle is listed as being part-owner of two of them. One suspects that here was a man ahead of his time—and that the yacht racing world was not yet ready for the idea of one-design racing!

SUSANNE was always a famously photogenic yacht and here is combined all the grace that Fife and the schooner rig can express in a yacht. She was built at a Y.R.A. Linear Rating of 79·07 by A. & J. Inglis of Glasgow in 1904 for a German owner, O. Huldschinsky of Kiel. She raced in the large handicap class and although her record does not appear to have been spectacular one feels she was always a spectacular boat. She did in fact win, under sealed handicap, the 1905 German Emperor's Cup for the race from Dover to Heligoland.

The photograph was taken in 1910 when she had been reclassed as 23 Metre International Rating, but by then the schooner rig had given way to the big cutters for racing purposes. Nevertheless the tremendous power of the schooner on a reach, urged on by the big 'ballooner' set between the masts and sheeted to the main boom is well demonstrated. Note also the loose-footed clew to the foresail.

Susanne was still to be seen in 1925 under the ownership of Robert MacAlpine jnr., and can be said to have led a glorious life and enhanced the yachting scene, as would any woman of startling beauty. (P. 112-113.)

CICELY was designed by William Fife and built by J. G. Fay & Co. Ltd. at Southampton in 1902 for Cecil Quentin. She was contemporary with the schooner Meteor III, who was designed and built for the Kaiser in America. Neither of these yachts was strictly a racing yacht in the terms of that day and age; both were intended as 'fast cruisers'. Nevertheless, both were magnificent vessels and were inevitably drawn into racing. Cicely set nearly 10,000 sq.ft. of sail and had a Linear Rating of 95·67. She first met Meteor III (120 feet on loadline, 27 feet beam and 15 feet draft) in German waters and proved herself much the superior of the two, particularly on the wind. This picture, taken in 1908, shows her in conditions in which she revelled, and on the point of sailing at which she excelled. Contemporary records state 'a truly remarkable vessel and pointed wonderfully high for a schooner'.

In her first season, 1902, she raced in the Baltic in company with the third Meteor, Clara, Lasca, Iduna, and Nordwest—the finest fleet of schooners ever raced. Cicely won every event. With the new International Rating Rule of 1906 she became 26·35 metres, thus qualifying for the largest class, and she continued to race under handicap. Although severely penalized she won many races, including two Emperor's Cups and the Jubilee Challenge Trophy, while she also set up a new Dover-Ostend record.

Susanne: Length O.A. 93.7 ft. Length W.L. 75.03 ft. Breadth 19.8 ft. Depth 10.25 ft. Tons T.M. 154.

Cicely: Length B.P. 113.6 ft. Length W.L. 98.85 ft. Breadth 23.4 ft. Depth 12.2 ft. Draft 14.0 ft. Tons T.M. 263.

*T*HIS photograph was taken in August 1906. BRITOMART had been built the year before to the design of Alfred Mylne for W. P. Burton at R. McAlister & Son, Dumbarton, on the Clyde, with a Linear Rating of 52 feet. CREOLE had by now been sailing and racing for sixteen years—the shot itself is of handicap racing in the larger class and Creole's age is betrayed by the old 'clipper' bow. Britomart was one of the two new '52 footers', the other being the Herreshoff designed Sonya, built in 1905. Britomart's first season was not all that successful—she finished third out of four boats. But in 1906 she strode into her own and topped the race results in the class with 21 first prizes. A point well worth making here is the intensity of the racing. In that year the '52 footers' raced 45 events in twelve weeks. In our days of weekend events few yachts of any size could boast this number of starts.
Creole had a Linear Rating of 61·74 feet and set a sail area of 4,279 sq. ft. She was designed by G. L. Watson and built by Forrest & Son at Wivenhoe in Essex in 1890 as a 40 Rater under the old Sail Area Rule. Her owner then was Lt.-Colonel Villiers Bagot. From 1893 she sailed in the handicap classes. Creole must have been a darling boat. Colonel Bagot was still racing her in 1900, when she is referred to in books as the 'famous old Creole', and in 1904 she won the German Emperor's Cup at Cowes. In 1929 Creole still appears in Lloyd's Register under Colonel Bagot's ownership—a partnership of forty years. (P. 116-117.)

*H*ERE is a close-up of close racing in the International 8 Metre Rating Class in 1909. This class had been brought into being by the International Conference in 1906. The rule probably found its fullest development in the lovely Stephens designed, Plym built Iskareen which, after the 1939-45 war, crowned her career with a record of just under 7¾ hours for the famous Round-the-Island ('once round the Isle of Wight') Race. Then it was a question of the perfect geometry of the Bermudan rig with genoa headsail. But of the early days with which we are concerned, it is in these 8 Metres that I find the sail plan alone less aesthetically pleasing to the eye than in latter day counterparts. These jackyarders are truncated affairs compared with the sky-grasping line of some of the other classes of the day. But no one could fault the shapeliness of these hulls, their foaming bows and clean wakes. The different heights of the spreaders is interesting if not outstandingly significant. I believe their spinnakers have already been hoisted in stops and tacked firmly down on deck—they were luffed in those days. What else can these be that show between the two jibs, standing parallel to the luffs?

Britomart: Length 63.0 ft. Length W.L. 47.0 ft. Breadth 13.2 ft. Tons T.M. 47.

Creole: Length 70.5 ft. Length W.L. 60.05 ft. Breadth 13.3 ft. Depth 10.1 ft. Tons T.M. 54.

*I*N the eyes of his people, King George V was a 'sailor king',
and in truth he was an enthusiastic and knowledgeable yachtsman.

THE library of the Royal Yacht Squadron. On the wall hangs a portrait of the Emperor Napoleon III, presented by the Emperor himself in 1862. Napoleon III was a member from 1858 to 1872. After his fall, his wife the Empress Eugénie crossed from France to the Isle of Wight in Sir John Burgoyne's yacht Gazelle.

*F*OR marine photography, and for that great artist Frank Beken, 1909 seems to have been a vintage year. Here he has caught the 15 Metres in characteristic pose. HISPANIA, the King of Spain's yacht, leads the fleet after just rounding the weather mark. The last boat of the five is about to bear away round the buoy but there may be a sixth behind D8! Already the jib-topsails are going to sleep in the dead wind of the jackyarders. Spinnaker booms are being swung out. Incidentally D8 has a man up the mast at the clew height of her jib topsail—so there is some drama under way. (P. 120-121.)

A fleet of 15 Metres hard on the wind with their jackyarders reaching for the sky must have been as fine a sight as anyone saw. The Spanish royal yacht HISPANIA leads with PAULA fine on her weather quarter as the five of them tack out from the shore in a fresh westerly breeze. The difference in cut of the jackyard topsails of the two leaders is a point of interest. Hispania's mitre seam is formed very low down in the sail with the majority of the seams running parallel to the footyard. Aboard Paula the seams are rectilineal to this spar and the mitre runs approximately horizontally from its clew outhaul. One would say that the second boat's is the better setting of the two. (P. 122-123.)

*T*HIS picture of NYRIA is somewhat misleading—but all is explained when one is told that it was taken in 1923 and Nyria was built in the winter of 1905/6. She was designed by C. E. Nicholson and constructed by his firm of Camper & Nicholson for Mr. Robert Young, a well known polo player! Mr. Young had actually taken up sailing at the beginning of the 1905 season when he purchased the large handicapper Merrymaid. Without further ado he fell for yacht racing—after all, these large yachts were both the height of form and fashion, and intensely thrilling to sail—and commissioned the new boat for the following season. Nyria was launched on the April 10, 1906, and had a Linear Rating of 80. Like her rival White Heather (83 Rater) she was heavily constructed for her day and was classed 20 years at Lloyd's. She was composite built—she had steel frames—teak planked, and her lead keel scaled 50 tons. She set 8,260 sq.ft. of canvas. These two raced through the season within seconds of each other and completely overshadowed Sir James Pender's Kariad, who was so disappointed that he got rid of her to the breakers' yard!
Nyria as she appears in this photograph—she was then owned by Mrs. Workman—shows her re-rigged in the manner of the J Class, which became general practice as soon as naval architects found out how to make the 'Marconi' mast stand. It is interesting because of the mixture of modern and ancient; the new 'leg of mutton', 'Marconi' (now called Bermudan) mainsail; the old arrangement of a multiplicity of headsails in the foretriangle taken from the great gaff cutters. This state of affairs was to continue until the invention of the genoa in the small 6 Metre class and the development of the quadrilateral jib therefrom for the J Class America's Cup racers.

Nyria: Length 98.0 ft. Length W.L. 73.72 ft. Breadth 20.2 ft. Depth 10.6 ft. Draught 13.0 ft. Tons T.M. 169.

CLOSE stuff among the 8 Metres in August 1911—in the days before kicking straps on the main boom and foreguys and uphauls on the spinnaker boom. These methods of controlling the sails were rather surprisingly slow to develop and it is a wonder that someone didn't think of sticking the heel of the spinnaker boom farther up the mast to get more spread in the sail as early as this. In Frank Beken's picture are two full-rigged ladies complete with wide hats and leg-of-mutton sleeves—even if the leg-of-mutton mainsail had not yet been invented. The foreground yacht is by Fife—identified by the 'dragon' head scroll on her bow. (P. 128-129.)

HERE's an agreeable picture of the schooner fleet in close formation. ADELA, 224 tons T.M.; METEOR I, owned by the Kaiser, 412 tons; GERMANIA, 368 tons; and CETONIA, formerly the Esperance, of 295 tons.
Germania was owned by Dr. Krupp von Bohlen und Halbach and was built in his own Krupp shipyard in 1903. Krupp was hardly a lesser personnage than the Kaiser himself—and these two fine schooners were there to prove that Germany was a maritime power to be reckoned with. Although there is a light wind of hardly as much as 10 knots these magnificent vessels heel to the breeze and sail with a bone in their teeth. Cetonia belonged to Lord Iveagh, the head of the Guinness clan, and was smaller than either of the two German yachts, yet still carried nearly 11,000 sq. ft. of sail. All four came from the boards of different designers Adela was by W. C. Storey and built by Fay's at Southampton; Meteor came from America; Germania was designed by Max Oertz; and Cetonia was Soper designed and built at Gosport by Camper & Nicholson. How many naval architects of our own generation can challenge this sort of commission—and how many shipyards now exist that are capable of translating their artistic gifts and experience into the terms of real sailing vessels? (P. 130-131.)

WE have several pictures of CREOLE racing with other yachts of her day, but none of them shows the boat off to such advantage as this one does. She was G. L. Watson designed in 1890 but the picture was taken in 1913—twenty-three years later— and she is as spruce and as well cared for as the day she went afloat. The gentleman for whom she was built, Colonel Villiers Bagot, owned her all through these years and with such a graceful yacht one can readily understand the care and consideration that the Colonel lavished on her. The set of her canvas can hardly be faulted and everything is 'shipshape and Bristol fashion'.

WE mention in our synopsis of early racing rules the importance of the year 1906 when the International Conference (from which the Americans chose to abstain) adopted a new uniform rule of measurement and also an agreement on scantlings. This picture was taken in 1909 and shows two yachts of the 6 Metre Class. These were the direct progenitors of the famous 'Sixes' of between the wars and indeed almost up to the present day—probably the finest small yachts for performance and ability at sea ever to come into being. Described by those who didn't realise what they were killing as 'pot-bellied lead mines', they became too expensive to live, although we are the poorer for their passing—just as we are the poorer for the vanishing of the great schooners and cutters with which this book is mostly concerned. Without Frank and Keith Beken many will not realise that these splendid creatures ever existed—with them, to some degree, the reader will be able to say 'Et in Arcadia ego'.

But here the 6 Metres are in their infancy. Who the two boats are we do not know, but they vary considerably. The one without a jackyarder, the one with; the one with quite a modern two-cockpit deck layout, the other with quite an International One Design cabin trunking. The one with graceful overhangs at bow and stern, the other with a nearly plumb stem and 'sawn-off' counter. And is that the 'first' genoa that the boat astern is carrying? The helmsman of the leading yacht is sailing in his waistcoat with a pipe clamped firmly between his teeth. Who is his fair companion with her 'Ascot Hat' held in place by a filmy silk scarf? With today's shorts and bright yellow lifejackets the Age of Elegance is gone!

*B*OTH these majestic yachts are the work of Fife. The picture was taken in 1911. The interesting thing is the comparison in size. WHITE HEATHER ahead and out on the lee bow of the yacht astern looks comparatively small and dainty compared with that magnificent schooner. Yet she was a sizeable vessel of 150 tons T.M. and there's a crew of over 20 on deck. Her Linear Rating was 82·60. And one wonders what happy mischance caused the sailmaker to sow the 'B' on back to front! Otherwise it is impossible to fault the perfection of that spread of canvas.

White Heather was built in 1904 at Fay's in Southampton for Myles B. Kennedy. By the time of the photograph she had passed into the ownership of H. B. L. Sedgwick. Seven years old, she still looks as if she had just stepped out of a band-box.

WATERWITCH had been built in the same year by the Ailsa S. C. Co., at Troon in Ayrshire, for G. Cecil Whitaker. The 'open' racing in 1904 was at a low ebb, but the large handicap class was graced by the appearance of this fine yawl. In the picture, of course, she appears as a cutter but this was seven years later—there was rather a vogue for the yawl rig at the time of her build.

White Heather turned out to be a fast vessel although she was at first deemed by the 'fancy' to be rather tender. In her second year she had a great season, winning the Royal London Yacht Club's race from Cowes to the Clyde, which took the large handicap class north, and —for good measure—won the return race south to Cowes sponsored by the Clyde Yacht Clubs. Incidentally, 1905 was a black year for Irish racing. The Royal Irish Yacht Club, with no prospect of securing even a small attendance of racing yachts, went so far as to abandon their regatta altogether. It was noted at the time that the first season in fifty years passed 'without a first class regatta at Kingston'.

White Heather was heavily built for a racing yacht of that era and was also classed at Lloyd's. In 1906 her chief rival was Nyria, an 80 Rater by Charles E. Nicholson—interestingly enough also ruggedly built to Lloyd's. The revolt against the comparatively lightly constructed racing machine which bore fruit in the 'Metre Rule' was obviously under way. The racing between White Heather and Nyria was remarkably close—White Heather allowing 2 minutes 41 seconds over a 40 mile course—and frequently winning by seconds. Myles Kennedy sold her after the 1906 season and built White Heather II at Fife's as a first class cutter. (P. 136-137.)

White Heather: Length 91.2 ft. Length W.L. 77.0 ft. Breadth 19.95 ft. Depth 11.2 ft. Tons T.M. 151.

Waterwitch: Length 120.0 ft. Length W.L. 96.0 ft. Breadth 26.6 ft. Depth 13.7 ft. Tons T.M. 352.

*T*HIS is a proud procession of 1910—the 12 Metres with JAVOTTE leading CINTRA, CYRA, ALACHIE, NARGIE and HERA. When talking about the 15 Metres we have referred to the 12 Metres as comparatively small boats. In a way they look much the same size in the pictures and in a way they were. The '12s' were only about 10 feet shorter, but they were some 27 tons Thames Measurement as against 50 tons—and, as Thames tonnage is more a measurement of volume than anything else, it will be seen that as yachts they were not much more than half the size of the '15s'!

Here the fleet look almost like early day One Designs—same hulls, same rigs, same sails! Although this is an impressive shot, it *does* show the great weakness of the gaff rig. Note the tremendous 'twist' in the mainsails and the whole sailplan aft of the mast. Take Javotte, the head yacht, for instance. It would appear that there is nearly 45 degrees difference in trim between the main boom and the spars aloft. (P. 138-139.)

*A*N idyllic picture of a summer's day's racing before the two 'Great' Wars—when all the world was young! Sun, a light breeze, a calm sea—and a close start. The leeward boat in the centre is the King of Spain's HISPANIA. The yachts look as though they were one-designs but that of course is far from the case. In the Department of Tactical Warfare, Hispania's situation appears pretty desperate. She certainly can't tack until everybody else does—but then of course she may not need to. Note that the jackyarders are set on the thin pole of the 'marconi' mast which must have added pure weight problems, apart from anything else, way up aloft. (P. 140-141.)

*S*ONYA was a Yank through and through. She was designed by Nathaniel Herreshoff to the 52 Linear Rating and built by Herreshoff Mfg. Co. at Bristol, Rhode Island in 1905 for Mrs. Turner-Farley, a noted British yachtswoman—as indeed were her daughters! Sonya was an interesting '52' to say the least and demonstrated a different design approach. She had the largest girth in the fleet, the smallest 'd' measurement and the shortest waterline. She was a very powerful boat and hard on her spars—she twice lost her mast in 1905. In the following year she was frequently in trouble, particularly with her gaffjaws.

As mentioned elsewhere, 1906 was the year of the Conference which established the new International Rating rule and it turned out that the '52's' were close alongside the new 15 Metre rating. So here is Sonya in 1911 under the ownership of Noel T. Kershaw C.B., running before a bright breeze in the van of the fleet—and all of them with as much sail as can be crammed on. That torn top batten pocket betrays a muscular wind with plenty of work for the crew on the windward leg. (P. 142-143.)

Sonya: Length 59.3 ft. Length W.L. 46.22 ft. Breadth 13.1 ft. Depth 7.3 ft. Tons T.M. 42.

HERE is a solo portrait of H.M. The King of Spain's HISPANIA. Hispania of the 15 Metre Class. She was Fife designed for her royal owner and was a 'regular' from the year of her build until the 'lights went out' all over Europe. Her sail spread was of the order of 4,300 sq.ft. The foredeck crew is busy running out the spinnaker boom in preparation for the next leg of the course as the helm goes up and the boat starts to bear away for the mark. The forehatch is open and the spi head is being pushed up on deck. There must have been quite an advantage in those old-fashioned luffed spinnakers in that you kept all your headsails up on the run so far as I can see and just handed the kite at the end of the downwind leg! Nowadays we get all tangled up in foreguys and afterguys and uphauls and rehoisting the genoa and getting it sheeted and clearing the spi sheets—and all sorts of knitting.

145

Arrow - 1854

(Colour Lithograph. T. G. Dutton after J. Taylor)

This valiant cutter is one of the pioneers of yacht racing. Her name, as well as that of her owner Joseph Weld, figures in the opening chapters of every history of yachting. Weld was a younger son but, when his brother took holy orders, he came into a considerable fortune which gave him the opportunity of indulging his passion for sailing. Arrow's lines were lifted from those of a French smuggler driven up on the English coast. She was built in 1821 and began her winning career by taking the Yacht Club's cup at Cowes in 1826. When finally she was beaten by the Pearl, Arrow was sold and subsequently passed some years in a mudberth. Eventually she was bought by a Mr. Tankerville, lengthened at the bow and put back into trim.

Dauntless and Cambria at the start of
the Transatlantic Race - 1870

(Colour Lithograph.
E. G. Dutton after R. L. Stopford)

A short time after the start Cambria (to windward)
and Dauntless lost sight of each other and did not meet
again until they reached the finishing line off New
York. After twenty-three days only a few hours separated the victrix Cambria from the second boat home.
Cambria's great victory made its impression for the
English cause in America but it didn't stop her being
beaten by the American fleet in the contest for the
America's Cup, the contest for which she had raced
and won across the Atlantic.

*T*HIS picture of WESTWARD was taken about a year after that on pages 154-155. It shows her power and majesty in conditions in which she was supreme, a strong breeze over the quarter. The other picture shows her sailing full-and-bye.

There is a similar photograph to this depicting the Fife schooner Susanne but fine ship as she is shown to be in the shot, she was a smaller vessel by some 20 feet and somehow lacks the ultimate and very regal authority that Westward demonstrates here. Susanne's International Rating was 23·21 metres; Westward's 29·09.

Running up Solent from the westward—appropriately enough!—in the sun-filled early afternoon she is doing all of 16 knots and pershaps more. If it hadn't been invented in the days of square riggers, this sight would have surely given birth to the phrase 'under a cloud of canvas'. With that big 'fisherman' set between the masts there cannot be a sail left in the locker except for storm canvas. There is a certain amount of gymnastics going on with the mast end of the spinnaker boom which incidentally is not all that many feet shorter than the main boom. I haven't the nerve to call a spar like that a spinnaker *pole !* (P. 148-149.)

*W*E have already seen WATERWITCH in another photograph in close company with the smaller White Heather of a mere 151 tons T.M. Waterwitch was Fife designed for Cecil Whitaker (Cicely) and built by Ailsa S. C. Co., at Troon in Ayrshire in 1911. After that, her story is a short one to say the least.

In the picture she is all power and grace and seemingly everything a first-rate schooner ought to be. However the fact remains that she only raced one season. Astoundingly she was then *broken up*—sent to the knackers, what you will. But not all of her! Her rig and other equipment was transferred Whitaker's new yacht, the 380-ton Margherita—but she was Nicholson designed and built.

Westward: Lenght O.A. 115.9 ft. Length W.L. 96 ft. Breadth 26.7 ft. Depth 17.9 ft. Tons T.M. 338.

Waterwitch: Length O.A. 120 ft. Length W.L. 96 ft. Breadth 26.6 ft. Depth 13.7 ft. Tons T.M. 352.

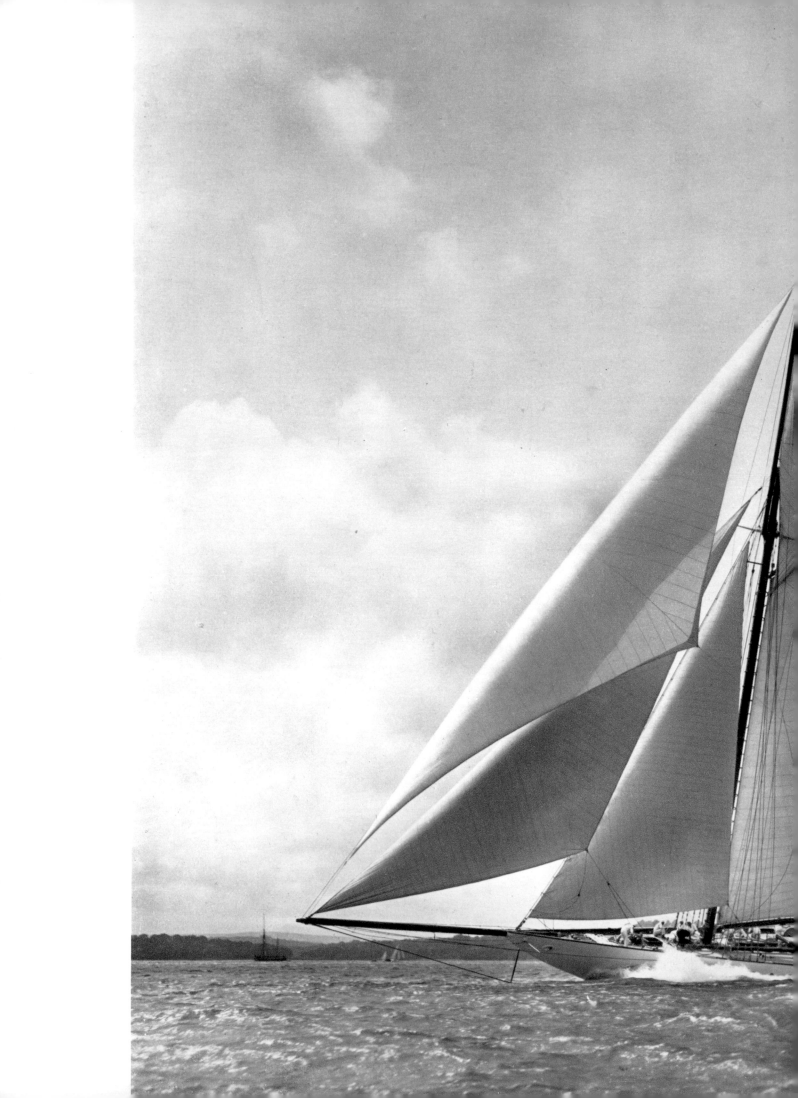

*T*HE Kaiser's METEOR III, to weather in this picture, was designed by Max Oertz and built in Kiel in 1909. GERMANIA was also Oertz designed, for Dr. Krupp von Bohlen und Halbach; she was the king of German industry's 'aye, aye, Sir' to his Kaiser. But old-fashioned remarks about old-fashioned wars apart, these two magnificent schooners exemplify one of the peaks of human artistry in the field of naval architecture. The point is that *these* yachts and their kinswomen will never be old-fashioned. In their way they will always be *ahead* of so-called modernity—in the manner that Michelangelo is closer to us than Annigoni, and Beethoven has more to say to the human race than the Beatles. One need say no more than this—and to add that Time is the great Thief. (P. 152-153.)

*W*HAT shall one say about WESTWARD? She was steel built. She set 12,000 sq.ft. of sail originally. Her beam was 27 feet. She was designed and built by Nathaniel G. Herreshoff, the 'Wizard of Bristol'—Bristol, Rhode Island—in 1910. This year brings us near to the end of the time period of this book. A war to change the world was on its way. But before visions of that disastrous, stupid and contemptible slaughter born of nothing but the deadly sin of pride rise up in front of our eyes, let us enjoy the gift of sight by gazing on one of the most beautiful of all man-made things—a great schooner under all plain sail.
Westward was first owned by Mr. A.S. Cochran who had as his racing skipper the redoubtable Charlie Bevis. In her first year, 1910, she started no more than eleven times and on each occasion crossed the finishing line first. In a strong quartering wind she was tremendously fast and practically unbeatable. She was sold before the outbreak of the Great War to the Verein See-fahrt Hamburg—the wealthy German syndicate which bought many large and costly yachts to make sport for their Emperor. She was then renamed Hamburg II and at that time carried 16,000 sq.ft. of canvas.
One might think that would be the end of the Westward story as an apocalypse swept away the foundations of wealth and society. But the hurricane of war passed through and one is happy to say that Westward survived to reappear in her old style. This is another story for another book, but after the death of her last owner, T. B. F. Davis, she left Dartmouth under tow of the tug Portwey on July 14, 1947, to be sunk in Hurd Deep. (P. 154-155.)

*A*s can be seen it was not all big stuff even as early as 1897. Small yacht sailing in boats of approximately the size of present day Dragons went on with great gusto. Here is a group of '24 footers' (Y.R.A. Linear Rating Rule) off Portsmouth—see how they were able to find time to paint the Spitheard forts in those days! The five leaders are THETIS (No. 7), SPEEDWELL, FAIRY, ANNETTA and IMVURA. Thetis has no battens in her mainsail. The next three have battened leaches and Imvura the weather boat, is really very 'outré'. She has three full-length, projecting battens in the lower half of the main and two more conven-

Westward: Length O.A. 115.9 ft. Length W.L. 96 ft. Breadth 26.7 ft. Depth 17.9 ft. Tons T.M. 338.

tional but still projecting ones in the upper half. There was no dearth of experiment fifty years ago. The second boat, Speedwell (No. 13), was owned by a redoubtable Miss Cox; perhaps that is her in the sailor's hat and the white blouse with the bouffoné sleeves. Speedwell was champion that year and was designed by Payne. In 1904 Miss Cox and Mrs Schenley were champions in a new '24' Duet. Which shows that even then, when they took to the sea the female of the species could be just as formidable as the male!

*T*HE 8 Metre was another class to come into being with the adoption of the International Rating Rule of 1906. Like their smaller sisters the 6's they lasted in a developed form right through to the Hitler War. In fact there was some racing to be had in the 8's immediately after the so-called Peace. The 'modern' 8 made a fine seaworthy cruising yacht of good performance. By then of course they had become much bigger and heftier yachts than those that you see here. There is little doubt from the attitudes of the crews that racing was as hot as cayenne pepper and a good deal closer than we sometimes get in present day keel classes. Again we see that ladies in what we might consider most inappropriate attire took part in the racing!

*T*HIS photograph of 1912 reminds us that yachting and yacht-racing before the Great War wasn't confined to the great cutters and schooners which shipped two or three dozen crew. QUAKER GIRL (K6) and GUENORA (K7) are International 7 Metres. They represent the Dragon Class of their day and, truth to tell, were not much different in dimensions or the crews they carried. Quaker Girl designed by A.R. Luke and built by Luke Brothers at Hamble in 1911 was one of the crack boats in the class.

There is a fresh breeze blowing as they leap from wave to wave in the Solent chop. They would

Quaker Girl and Guenora: Length T.M. 32 ft. Length W.L. 23.25 ft. Beam 6.4 ft. Draft 4.17 ft. Sail Area 690 sq. ft.

have been planing if planing had been invented in those days! However, as one can see, these small yachts did not lack for seaworthy virtues. Their rig shows that when one reefed, the gaff was set lower alongside the mast, thus relieving windage and making the staying of the mast a very simple affair. Quaker Girl, like Guenora, is well reefed down and the peak is hardly three feet above the truck. With full sail set it would be a good six feet farther aloft. The working of the spinnakers is still stone age stuff, but nevertheless one notes the downhaul to prevent the spinnaker boom skying. One may also remark that with the advent of horizontally cut mainsails, battens had come to stay. In spite of the fresh conditions these two boats must have had a great race to windward for them to be in the relative positions that we see in the picture. The crews are very elegant with their white hats, jerseys and bell-bottom trousers—no shapeless oilskins spouting water here!

Quaker Girl belonged originally to the brothers Luke. She was sold just before the 1914-18 war to a 'name' helmsman, Basil Lubbock. After the war when the 7 Metre class had disappeared from the scene, she turned up in Scandinavia.

*G*ERMANIA was a fine vessel, designed by Max Oertz and built at Krupp Germania Werft for her owner Dr. Krupp von Bohlen und Halbach. She is on record as having maintained a speed of 15 knots over 5 nautical miles so she was certainly not a slow boat.

The major interest of this design is however not so much in her merits as the superb yacht which this photograph shows her to be, or in her prowess on the racing scene of which there is not much evidence; it lies in her unspoken comment on the life and times of European Society in the short years before the roof fell in.. To generalize, it all went back to the ambitions of the House of Hohenzollern which had unseated Hapsburg domination of Germany and whose members were determined to prove that they were as good as their relatives who 'owned' the British Empire. It all sounds petty and old-fashioned today, but with his near relation, the Prince of Wales, taking an active, successful, and popular interest in the sport of yacht-racing, with Britannia ruling the waves and with his determination to make the Imperial German Navy the equal of and if possible the superior to the might of British sea-power, the Emperor Wilhelm II plunged into the business of conquest at Cowes and similar places.

He bought and fitted out Thistle, who though fast for her day had raced against America in 1851 and unsuccessfully challenged Volunteer for 'the Cup' in 1887. He re-christened her Meteor but she was naturally no match for the new Britannia and Valkyrie. He then got the Scottish designer G. L. Watson to design him a 20 Rater which he built in Kiel as Vineta, which he gave away to a noble relative. In 1896 Watson designed and Henderson in Glasgow built Meteor II for him. She was probably the best yacht Watson ever designed. Under a British skipper and crew she won every race before leaving for Kiel. But the 'power had gone elsewhere' and interest was centred on British-American rivalry, so Wilhelm II got precious little of the kudos which was going, and in 1901 he turned his masterpiece of a yacht over to the German Navy under the name Orion. In a move to outflank his kinsman he ordered the 412 ton Meteor III from America, and in order to encourage his nation as a 'sport and sea-loving people' raced her mostly in his own waters. During the careers of the first three Meteors all the handling —or by far the greater part—was carried out by British crews, but in 1907-9 the time had come to cease dependence on foreigners. The magnates of German industry were enlisted in this fight for national prestige—hence came the schooner Germania (366 tons T.M.) which belonged, as we have said, to Krupp von Bohlen. The Emperor himself had the superb

400-ton schooner, Meteor IV, built at the Germania yard to designs of Max Oertz (one appreciates the niceties of the grading of the tonnages of these magnificent vessels) and when she sailed she was all German manned under German command. For all that, Germania was the most successful of the two.

Germania: Length O.A. 122 ft. Length W.L. 107 ft. Breadth 27 ft. Depth 13 ft. Tons T.M. 366.

ONCE more we have a photograph of the schooners when racing in their prime. The weather yacht is the giant GERMANIA of Dr. Krupp, measuring 366 tons Thames Measurement. To leeward of her is the much smaller Fife designed SUSANNE, still nevertheless 154 tons T.M. A cursory glance at the photograph might lead one to suppose that they were of similar dimensions. But Gemania is farther away from the camera and her hull length is the same if you put a rule on them. Astern comes CICELY of 263 tons. Perhaps this was one of those 'small boat's races', as we call them today! A day when the big ones can't shake the little ones off in the light breeze and a calm sea. True the larger boats carry their way farther, but the tiddlers get moving faster—not that Susanne could be called a tiddler. But there isn't enough muscle in the wind to give the upper sails proper shape and most of the crews are down to leeward. (P. 162-163.)

TWO fine 15 Metres race in brisk conditions inside the Isle of Wight. MARISKA leads with a reef in her main and her topsail along her lee deck. She was Fife designed and built in 1908. Here in 1912 note the 'Marconi' mast and how naturally the Bermuda mainsail must have developed as soon as the naval architects had solved the staying problems. The 15 Metres measured some 50 tons T.M. so they were quite a lot bigger than the 12's of today's America's Cup races. They must have been exciting boats to sail in these conditions— and the cutter rig has always seemed to set a hull off better than the sloop, at any rate to the eye of the beholder. (P. 164-165.)

IT was Cecil Whitaker who owned the splendid Fife designed Fay built 263 ton schooner Cicely (later Lamorna) in 1909. In 1913 he was the owner of an even longer and more splendid schooner MARGHERITA. We are looking at her now. She was, all 380 tons of her, the creation of the great Charles E. Nicholson and was built by his firm, Camper & Nicholson. Her length overall was 161 feet.
But in 1914 there was to be the great interruption in yacht racing, and in the growth and development which held so much promise. Margherita was however a 'yacht' in the best traditions of that old-fashioned name. She appeared after the war under the ownership of S. B. Joel and in 1925 was sold by Camper & Nicholson to Sir William Reardon. In later years she was a three-masted schooner. Her last listing under this name in Lloyd's was in 1932.
What a sight she must have been on the morning that this photograph was taken. Even though there's only a comparatively light breeze blowing she is using all her waterline length and must be moving through the dancing waters at something like 12 knots with all her canvas except a spinnaker set. It appears that there is even a main topmast staysail drawing behind that big loose-footed 'fisherman'. This was yachting in the grand style. Careful examination reveals

at least 36 men aboard and that included the single, sentinel figure at the foremast futtocks, standing hand on hip enjoying the view from some seventy feet above deck. The king-spoke of the wheel stands as tall as the quartermaster himself.

There is an English translation of a poem by François Villon which runs.

> *The wind has blown them all away*
> *The good, the bad, the foul, the fair—*
> *Where are the snows of yesteryear.*

This breeze of 1913, sweet and gentle as it may have been on this summer day in June, was blowing vessels like Margherita away for ever.

Margherita: Length O.A. 133 ft. Breadth 25.0 ft. Depth 15 ft. Tons T.M. 380.

*T*HIS photograph is extremely interesting from the point of view of a yachting historian. It was taken in 1913. Britomart and Sonya had been the two new '52 footers' (Y.R.A. Linear Rating) of 1905. In 1906 the International Conference had agreed the International Rating Rule which for practical purposes transformed the '52 footers' into the new 15 Metre classification. This shot of ISTRIA (D7) five years later shows the fresh development in the 15 Metre Class which brought in the pronounced type of bow and stern overhang. This feature became the model of the later 'Shamrocks'.

The photograph also shows the introduction of the 'Marconi' mast, with the topsail laced to the mast instead of being set on a jackyard. To make this 'toothpick' stand, the rigging had to be carried way aloft. Outriggers were introduced at the chain plates to give sufficient spread to support the topmast rigging. Observe the additional sparring height of Istria over D10 and her train-bearers. Modern 'boats' (as opposed to 'yachts') would hardly think of reefing in wind conditions which must have been about 15 knots on this day—but then they aren't as tall-sticked, and do they go as fast? (P. 168-169.)

*T*HESE two 15 Metres off Ryde in 1911, VANITY and SOPHIE ELIZABETH, epitomise the sleek perfection and grace of these fine 50 tonners. It was this class which brought the International Rating Rule to its very peak. It must be remembered that the 12 Metres were considered rather small boats. The 15 Metre yachts were that much larger and yet they did not outrage the imagination with the 'improbability' of the 19 and 23 Metres! The perfect proportions of rig to hull, the clean planes of the sail plan, and the artistry of the sailmakers working in Egyptian cotton—these are all demonstrated in this photograph in a way that will never be seen again.

It is a point of minor interest that Vanity, the leading yacht, has her jackyarder hoisted to leeward of her main-gaff halyard system on this tack while her rival's is set to weather. Both were designed by the master hand of Fife.

*L*AMORNA we have been before. She was the Fife designed and Fay built Cicely of 1902—the schooner who in her first season and in Baltic waters won every race in the finest schooner fleet afloat; Meteor II, Clara, Lasca, Iduna and Nordwest.

She was another of the long-lived ones, for she last appears in Lloyd's fifty years after her launching (49 to be exact, but 50 is a good round number). Mind you, in order to last that number of years a good deal of 'surgery' had to be done. Of Britannia it was said that little of the original structure remained at the end of her life. In Lamorna's lifetime she certainly had her stern post and part of her deadwood renewed. Her bottom planking was renewed in teak in 1922, her decks were renewed, also in teak, in 1933. This 1913 photograph was being used in brokerage advertising in 1933, which makes one wonder a bit!

I never saw her rigged but can recall to this day her hull lying off Camper & Nicholson's yard at Gosport in the early years after the 1939-45 war. She then had a black hull and what John Nicholson, now Chairman of the company, called a 'half-dollar gold line'. This combination set off to perfection the beauty of Lamorna's sheerline, into which all the skill and artistry of Fife's hand seemed to have been concentrated. She had in particular a most beautiful bow profile—with the most accurately balanced of lines between the fiddle or clipper bow and what was rather depressingly called the spoon bow. The only other yacht design genius who demonstrated this touch was Nat Herreshoff.

Lamorna: Length 13.6 ft. Length W.L. 98.06 ft. Breadth 23.3 ft. Depth 12.2 ft. Tons T.M. 263.

MARIQUITA and CORONA were of the 19 Metre strain. These 100 tons T.M. vessels might well have developed into a great class. They were just that little less 'improbable' than the greatest of the great cutters. They were good examples to the International Metre Rule but their life was to be fairly short. Both Mariquita and Corona were built in 1911. Corona was owned by Almeric Paget M.P.—later Lord Queenborough and a great flag officer of the Royal Thames Yacht Club—and Richard Hennesey. Mariquita was owned by A.K. Stothert. Octavia (William Burton) was also a 19 Metre.

Corona was to be one of the testbeds for the post-war development of the 'Marconi' (now Bermudan rig). In 1928, under the ownership of H. A. Andrae, she was racing with one of those tall masts with diamond rigging, the first step towards the sailplans that we know today.

Mariquita: Length 81.8 ft. Breadth 17 ft. Depth 9.8 ft. Tons T.M. 100.

*I*ERNE and ALACHIE are here photographed off Le Havre in the summer of 1914—and racing at speed. There seems a slight divergency of opinion as to how much sail to carry. The leeward yacht has her jib topsail set while her rival's fore triangle is bald-headed above her jib. Both seem to be going as fast as each other. But of course it may be a question of the balance of either of these yachts, the amount of helm carried and the ease or difficulty of steering. The jackyarders on the Marconi masts have now got themselves a small batten to help the leech stand.

As these are the 12 Metres and 12 Metres in their developed form are the largest class racing yachts of today—even if they *do* only race for the America's Cup—and as this was to be the last Summer of Peace for many a long year, we close our book here. (P. 176-177.)

SUMMARY OF RATING RULES

From 1852 to 1875: The Rule in general use was that of the Royal Thames Yacht Club. This was a *Tonnage Rule*. One spoke of a boat and classified her by her Thames Tonnage or Tons Thames Measurement, or Tons T.M. — e.g. a '40 Tonner'.

From 1875 to 1882: The Yacht Racing Association took on the administration of yacht racing rules. The Y.R.A. based its writ originally on the Royal Thames Yacht Club rule which in its turn went back to the regulations of the Revenue as applied to vessels of the merchant marine.

From 1882 to 1886: The rule was modified but was still based on tonnage. This is perhaps best identified by the phrase *R.Y.A. Tonnage Rule* in Lloyd's Register and other documentation.
The formula was:

$$\frac{(L + B)^2 \times B}{1730} = \text{Tons Racing}$$

Again in the vocabulary of the day, one continued to speak of tonners—e.g. a '10 Tonner Y.R.A.'.

From 1887 to 1895: The Rule was scrapped and its whole basis was entirely changed. Between these years ran the writ of the *Sail Area Rule*. The formula was:

$$\frac{L \times \text{Sail Area}}{6000} = \text{Rating}$$

Now one talked, for instance, of '20 Raters'.

From 1896 to 1905: *The Sail Area Rule* was now transformed into a new rule—the Linear Rating Rule.
The formula was:

$$\frac{L + B + \tfrac{3}{4}G + \tfrac{1}{2}\sqrt{\text{S.A.}}}{2} = \text{Rating in feet}$$

One spoke of a '52 Footer'.

From 1906 onward: The rule of the International Conference—the *International Metre Rule* held sway. Even the America's Cup to-day is raced for by 12 Metres to a modified version of this rule.

INDEX
TO ILLUSTRATIONS AND COMMENTARY

(Entries in capital letters indicate an illustration. The figures in brackets
which follow indicate the pages on which the illustrations can be found)